To Albert,

From
        the Petersons.
            Xmas   1947.

ASTROLOGY FOR EVERYONE

What It Is and How It Works

BY EVANGELINE ADAMS

Author of "THE BOWL OF HEAVEN," "ASTROLOGY: YOUR
PLACE IN THE SUN," *and* "ASTROLOGY: YOUR
PLACE AMONG THE STARS"

THE BLAKISTON COMPANY

PHILADELPHIA

CIRCLE BOOKS EDITION PUBLISHED
BY ARRANGEMENT WITH DODD, MEAD & COMPANY, INC.

CIRCLE BOOKS is a series published by
The Blakiston Company, 1012 Walnut St., Philadelphia 5, Pa.

CL

PRINTED IN THE UNITED STATES OF AMERICA

TO MY CLIENTS

A DEDICATION AND AN APPRECIATION

FACING me across the desk on which I am writing these words is a chair which I call my Seat of the Mighty. In it and in its now decrepit predecessors nearly a hundred thousand people have sat.

John Burroughs has sat in that chair; so have James J. Hill and William Jennings Bryan and Enrico Caruso and the late J. Pierpont Morgan and Richard Harding Davis and Jospeh Jefferson and Lillian Nordica and Lady Paget and Hezekiah Butterworth and Minot J. Savage. Do you wonder that to me it has been, and still is, a Seat of the Mighty?

If you have never had your horoscope read it may seem strange to you that these great personages should come to Evangeline Adams to ask advice as to how to make money, how to make love, how to make happiness. If I were not so firmly convinced of astrology's infallibility, I too might wonder. But no matter how much or how little they have learned from me, there is no limit to the amount which I have learned from them.

I remember asking Mr. Hill how he went about building a railroad. "Well," he said, "not at all the way you think. First I see in my mind's eye the two places that need to be connected: what kinds of places they are, what kinds of people live in them and what kinds of businesses they are engaged in. Then I see the country in between: the cities and towns and rural sections and the kinds of people who live there. Then I see the rails being made, the stations being built, the trains stopping at the stations, the people getting

v

on and off. But not until the whole thing is so much a part of my consciousness that I can hear the whistles blow do I build the railroad!"

Visualization! That is the theory on which Mr. Hill proceeded. At that time even our psychologists had not given it a name. But it was not the scientific lesson in his words which interested me. It was the human lesson: that the failure is the man who goes off half-cocked and that the successful man is he who does nothing of importance until he has made that thing a reality on the mental plane.

But not all my big lessons have been learned from big men. Way back in 1905, when I was practising in the Hotel Copley in Boston, a spinster milliner from a small town in New Hampshire visited me at a time when she was coming under aspects that would naturally depress her business. When I told her that she must not be surprised if the millinery trade was temporarily poor, she replied, "Oh, I know how to stir that up. I never allow my business to get dull."

She then told me that she owned a pack of cards, on each of which she had written the name of one of her customers. As soon as her patronage showed signs of falling off she took out these cards and went over them very slowly, visualizing distinctly the woman whose name was on the card at which she was looking; picturing her walking down the street and up the path to her door; and of course buying a new hat. Invariably, she said, within a day or two a sufficient number of her customers put in an appearance to make her as busy as she cared to be. In short, she practised the theory of vibrations.

I never know, when my door opens, the width or the depth of my caller's knowledge of life. James J. Hill and the theory of visualization—that was a natural and understandable association; but this little New England milliner and the far more abstruse theory of vibrations—well, after thirty-five years of such experiences I have learned to sit at the feet of every man and woman whom I find opposite me in the Seat of the Mighty.

And to them, my clients, in grateful affection I dedicate this book.

Evangeline Adams

Carnegie Hall,
New York, N. Y.

"What chariots, what horses
Against us shall bide,
While the stars in their courses
Do fight on our side?"

—KIPLING:
"The Astrologer's Song."

YOUR STARS

AND HOW TO KNOW THEM

An Introduction

THIS book attempts to tell in simple, untechnical language what astrology is and how it works.

It will help to refresh our memory, I believe, if we think of the heavens as a great circle, divided into equal parts, just as the face of a clock is divided by the numerals which mark the hours, or as a wheel is divided by its spokes. Each of these twelve divisions may be said to represent one of the twelve signs of the Zodiac: Aries the Ram, Taurus the Bull, Gemini the Twins, Cancer the Crab, Leo the Lion, Virgo the Virgin, Libra the Scales, Scorpio the Scorpion, Sagittarius the Archer, Capricorn the Goat, Aquarius the Water-bearer and Pisces the Fishes.

Astrology teaches us that there are also twelve types of individuals corresponding, roughly speaking, to these twelve signs. If you were born when the Sun was in Aries, the first sign, you are one kind of person; if you were born when it was in Scorpio, the eighth sign, you are another. Of course, there are other and finer distinctions. Not all of the hundreds of thousands or millions of people born strongly under the influence of one sign are the same. That would make life too easy, and too uninteresting! But it *is* true that each of these signs has definite characteristics, and that persons born under a certain sign take on a good many of the characteristics of that sign.

For example, *if you were born between March 22nd and*

April 20th of any past year, you are an Aries person, a "native" of the first sign, Aries the Ram. Aries people are leaders, pioneers, idealists, the Sir Galahads of the world. Consistency is not their virtue, and they are inclined to start new things before they finish the old. They are, however, ambitious, high-spirited, generous and chivalrous—they have great possibilities, if only they know enough about themselves to realize them.

If you were born between April 21st and May 21st, you are a Taurus person. Taurus is the second sign of the Zodiac and is symbolized by the Bull. Taurians like the good things of life, especially the good substantial things like food and drink and creature comforts. They are very fond of the home. They adore children. In love they are inarticulate and undemonstrative. In business they have force rather than finesse. In their domestic life, they are agreeable and usually calm and self-controlled—but don't take the latter trait too much for granted. It is never safe to wave the red flag in front of the bull!

If you were born between May 22nd and June 21st, you are a Gemini person. Gemini is the third sign of the Zodiac and is symbolized by the Twins. Its natives are often brilliant, versatile, flexible and changeable; sometimes dilettantes, often flirts, Gemini people are in truth twins—Castor and Pollux. The two sides of their character war with each other. They have turbulent minds; they make sudden digressions; they are annoyingly unexpected. But they are charming and stimulating. Their own mental agility generates mental agility in others. Their social success is assured. Their business success depends on their cultivation of self-control and concentration.

If you were born between June 22nd and July 23rd, you are a Cancer person. Cancer is the fourth sign of the Zodiac and is symbolized by the Crab. As a matter of fact, Cancer is much better than it sounds. Cancer is the domestic sign. Cancer people love their home and are expert in all matters concerned with it. They are sensitive and thin-skinned; suffer greatly from fancied slights; are apt to worry and be nervous, even fretful; they crave change and adventure; but at heart they are home-loving and home-making. And in love they are tenacious and loyal, once their affections are fixed.

If you were born between July 24th and August 23rd, you are a Leo person. Leo is the fifth sign of the Zodiac and is symbolized by the Lion. It is sometimes called the royal sign and those who are born under it are kings in the little court which they set up for themselves. If they aren't, they think they are! For Leo people love adulation, and if they don't get it, they imagine it. They possess, however, along with this minor weakness, many elements of strength. They are loyal, generous, high-minded, industrious to the point of immolation, and willing to give themselves to the utmost for those they love. Leo people seldom harbor grudges, and never stoop to anything petty or mean. They are big, fine, strong—like the lions they *are* and the kings they *would* be.

If you were born between August 24th and September 23rd, you are a Virgo person. Virgo is the sixth sign of the Zodiac and is symbolized by the Virgin. Virgo is an intellectual sign; and Virgo people are more intellectual than emotional. Their chief failing is that they are too critical of themselves and of others. This makes for unhappiness and misunderstanding. It is also difficult for them to express the affection that they feel. On the other hand, they are excellent conversationalists, brilliant in repartee, interested in many things, and on the whole most agreeable companions. They dislike inharmony and can always be counted on the

side of peace. They are inclined to be over-systematic and
"set" in their ways.

*If you were born between September 24th and October
23rd,* you are a Libra person. Libra is the seventh sign of
the Zodiac and is symbolized by the Scales. Libra is the sign
of symmetry, of balance, of beauty. Libra people are sociable, gay, often talented, and frequently artistic. They
are inclined to experiment with life rather than grapple with
it, to become charming drifters and beloved vagabonds.
They will yield on unimportant matters rather than cause
any disturbance or disagreeableness in the lives of those with
whom they are associated. But they have it in them to take
a firm stand. Once the Libra scales are set, look out!

*If you were born between October 24th and November
22nd,* you are a Scorpio person. Scorpio is the eighth sign
of the Zodiac and is symbolized by the Eagle and the Scorpion. These two symbols, the soaring eagle and the stinging
scorpion, are typical of the range of Scorpio persons. The
less developed nature of this sign is jealous, tyrannical, quick
to anger and hot for revenge. The highly developed Scorpio
person, like the late beloved Theodore Roosevelt, turns this
tremendous force into a passion for hard work and for worth-
while accomplishment. If you were born under this most
powerful of all the signs of the Zodiac, make sure that you
master its strength instead of being mastered by it. Be the
eagle, not the scorpion.

*If you were born between November 23rd and December
22nd,* you are a Sagittarius person, and the symbol of your
sign is the Man with an Arrow or Centaur. The symbol suggests directness and so does the sign. Sagittarians are frank,
open, honest to the point of bluntness, inclined to be brusque
and lacking in tact, but on the whole really splendid people.
Their blunt ways often rob them of the popularity which
should be theirs. (A good many bachelors and old maids

are found with Venus in this sign.) But underneath their brusque exterior they possess most of the sterling virtues and make splendid partners either in marriage or business. The typical Sagittarian has the virtues of his faults. He is unselfish, fearless, loyal, understanding. At his best, he is an 'dealist—a young man who sees visions and an old man who dreams dreams.

If you were born between December 23rd and January 20th, you are a Capricorn person. Capricorn is the tenth sign of the Zodiac and is symbolized by the Goat. It is used in astrological language to signify praiseworthy tenacity, the ambition to climb from crag to crag, the ability to overcome life's obstacles. All these traits are true of highly developed Capricorn people. I cannot say so much for those who are less developed. Capricorn, like Scorpio, is a sign which covers a very long range. If you were born under its influence, see to it that you keep your feet on the top rungs of the ladder. Be the goat of ancient symbolism, not the goat of modern slang.

If you were born between January 21st and February 19th, you are an Aquarius person. Aquarius is the eleventh sign of the Zodiac and is symbolized by the Man pouring water. It is considered by many the finest sign of the whole twelve. (Of course *I* think so, because I was born under it!) Eighty per cent of the people in the Hall of Fame are said to have been born under this sign. Its characteristics are well represented by its symbol. Aquarians "pour out"— they give themselves to the world, they are more interested in others than they are in themselves, they are impersonal, universal, cosmic in all their attitudes and reactions. This quality sometimes makes them unsatisfactory as lovers. Wives come to me and complain that their husbands are more infatuated with a school or a hospital or a cause than they are with them. But they are loyal friends and, in all really big matters, unselfish and dependable husbands and wives.

If you were born between February 20th and March 21st, you are a Pisces person. Pisces is the last of the twelve signs of the Zodiac and is symbolized by the Two Fishes, one swimming upstream and the other downstream. The symbol tells the story of the sign. Pisces people are agreeable companions, charming in manner and interesting in mind. They are generous to a fault, often without regard to wisdom, and are popular both at home and abroad. When it comes to practical matters, however, they are apt to be dreamers; they may even be drifters. First they swim upstream, then down. They don't seem to be able to make up their minds which fish they wish to follow. Of course, they *can* if they wish to. They have fine minds and finer instincts. They love beauty and desire to attain it. All they need is the right kind of guidance from the right kind of husband or wife— or, failing that, the right kind of astrologer!

There! That completes the twelve signs, except that I should add a brief statement in regard to the "cusps." A period of about seven days, when the vibrations of—for example—Sagittarius are merging into those of Capricorn, and Capricorn still retains some of the influences of Sagittarius, is known as the cusp. People born during this period will partake of the magnanimity and impulsiveness of Sagittarius and the conservatism and seriousness of Capricorn. In short, they are a combination of the two; and in order to understand thoroughly all the influences to which they are subject, they should take into consideration the characteristics of both signs. Those born at any other time in the astrological month need pay no attention to the cusps, which, in all probability, will not be referred to again in these pages.

A much longer and more thorough analysis of each sign is given in the chapters that follow; and in each case this longer description is supplemented by a series of three Solar Horoscopes, which apply specifically to you according to the part of the sign in which you were born. To get the full value from this information about the signs you should read, first, the general description, and, then, the Solar Horoscope of the person in whom you are interested.

So much for the signs. Now I ask you to recall that clock-like figure of the heavens, and to think if you will of second, minute and hour hands passing over the surface of the clock from one division to another just as the hands of a clock pass from one hour to another.

These hands of the celestial clock are luminous bodies which, more than any other astrological factors, make each individual horoscope different from every other. They are, in short, the Sun, the Moon, Mercury, Venus, Mars, Jupiter, Saturn, Uranus and Neptune. And they each have characteristics and influences as distinctive from each other as the characteristics and influences of the twelve signs.

Some of these "hands" move very slowly. These are the hour hands. Some move faster. These are the minute hands. Some move very fast. These are the second hands. The Moon is a second hand. It stays in one sign between two and three days only. It gets all around the twelve signs in about twenty-eight days. The Sun is a minute hand. It stays in one sign, roughly speaking, a month. It gets all the way around in one year. Some of the others stay several months or severals years in one sign. They are the hour hands.

These movements of the planets—for simplicity's sake, we will include the Sun and the Moon in this category—through the signs constitute the basis of all astrological calculation. Their position at the moment a person was born determines the horoscope.

There are, of course, details. When a planet comes into

a sign, its influence on us is modified by the characteristics of that sign. The Sun, for instance, is still the Sun, whether it is in Aries or in Scorpio; it still gives, life, health, vitality, strength: but the way it does its work is influenced greatly by the fact that Aries is a highly mental sign and Scorpio a highly physical one. Moreover, it is affected, as all the other planets are, not only by the sign in which it happens to be at the moment, but by the favorable or unfavorable relation in which it happens to be to its fellow planets.

If it weren't for the planets and these facts about them, it would be quite possible to determine, simply by knowing the astrological month in which a person was born, whether he or she would make a desirable partner—matrimonially or otherwise. As a matter of fact, there *are* certain marriages which have been traditionally regarded as biologically correct. Under this system, Aries people should be married to Leo or Sagittarius; Taurus to Virgo or Capricorn; Gemini to Libra or Aquarius; Cancer to Scorpio or Pisces; Leo to Aries or Sagittarius; Virgo to Taurus or Capricorn; Libra to Gemini or Aquarius; Scorpio to Cancer or Pisces; Sagittarius to Aries or Leo; Capricorn to Taurus or Virgo; Aquarius to Gemini or Libra; and Pisces to Cancer or Scorpio. And there is some reason, on the ground of natural congeniality between the signs, for these traditional groupings.

But to be accurate on so delicate and important a matter, you should know more than just the month in which a person was born. You should know the year, month, day, and, if possible, the hour and place, because only in that way can you tell where *all* the planets were at the time.

It makes a great deal of difference, for example, in this matter of love and marriage where Venus was at the moment you were born. Take Napoleon. He was a Leo person —that is, the Sun was in Leo at the time he was born—and in his public career he lived up royally to his royal sign; but his Venus happened to be in Cancer, and in his personal life, he showed himself to be a typical Venus-in-Cancer person: self-indulgent, comfort loving, and so fond of the pleasures of the table that he met his death from over-eating. Venus-in-Gemini people run equally true to form. They resent any kind of demonstration. They do not wish to be touched. We have all seen babies, one and two years old, who hate to be hugged and kissed. Nine times out of ten, their Venuses are in Gemini.

Where the planets happen to be from time to time *after* you are born is also important; not only their position in your own horoscope but in the astrological heavens as they affect the whole world. No one knows this latter fact better than I do, for when the planets are unfavorable, I get questions about strikes, riots, and threats of revolution in the industrial world; or else my clients bombard me with tales of family quarrels, feuds over property, divorces, and so on. If the planets are in certain other positions, I know I am going to have an avalanche of letters from people who are all stirred up about love!

So you can see that if the positions of the planets are so important in the life of a professional astrologer, they must be very important also in your own life. It behooves you, therefore, to know something about them. And as you see, it is very simple.

The main thing to keep in mind is that clock-like picture of the heavens which I have already given. I don't wish to bore you by repetition. But I cannot say too often that the astrological heavens are like the face of a great clock, and that the planets are like the second, minute and hour hands of that clock. I know it will help you to remember them that way.

In fact, that's all you do need to remember: that the heavens are divided into twelve parts, as the clock is: and that the planets are moving through these parts, as the hands of a clock do, at varying rates of speed.

Or, to turn to my other favorite figure; the heavens are like a great glass dome divided, as the horoscope chart is divided, into twelve segments representing the twelve signs of the Zodiac. Each of these segments is of a different astrological color; and all are continuously moving, passing and repassing, shedding rays of varying strength and color and power.

No one can stop this procession of the signs. No one can affect the movements of the planets through them. No one can soften or strengthen the shadings of their influence. All the astrologer can do, so far as the individual is concerned, is to show him how he can best take advantage of these influences—and the later ones to which he will inevitably be subject throughout his life.

But that is a great deal. It may mean the difference between success and failure, between happiness and unhappiness, between sickness and health throughout our whole lives.

In this chapter, I do not need to describe each of the planets and its effect on mankind. These descriptions are given in the next several pages. But I do not wish to leave the subject at this point without giving you one universally known example which will, I hope, clarify the whole problem. That example is the horoscope of the United States.

Certainly, nations have horoscopes—just as people do! France was born on such and such a date; Italy on another; Germany on still another; and our own country, as every American knows, on the fourth or July, 1776. All an astrologer needs to know to draw a horoscope of anybody or anything is this information about the birthday. It is better, of course, if she also knows the place and the hour; and in these matters, too, it is possible to achieve scientific accuracy so far as the United States is concerned. For it is generally accepted—and properly so, I believe—that the life of the American nation dates from that moment in Philadelphia at 3:03 in the morning, when the signers of the Declaration of Independence reached a positive decision to declare to the world their independence of England.

The Sun was in Cancer when the United States was born, but Gemini, the third sign of the Zodiac, was "rising," as we astrologers say, at the moment of birth, and is, therefore, most influential in determining our destiny. Gemini is itself a very nervous, restless, versatile, and highly mental sign. The fact that the United States was born so strongly under its influence would be enough, according to astrology, to account for much which is significant in American character and history. But that is not all. The ruling planet of the sign Gemini is Mercury, "The Messenger of the Gods," which governs the mind, the imagination, and the nerves. This combination of celestial influences explains why we are the world's greatest travelers, greatest advertisers, greatest salesmen—and why, incidentally, we are so subject to the American disease of "nerves."

Several important and influential planets were in the ascendant at the time this child among nations was born: among them, Mars, Venus and Jupiter. Mars is not only the God of War, but it is the planet which gives ambition, initiative, courage and aggressiveness. It is not difficult, therefore, to see how this intrepid planet has placed its mark on our countrymen. Venus, although popularly known as the Goddess of Love, performs many other gracious duties in the astrological scheme of things. She governs musicians, painters, actors, and artists in general—and surely no modern nation has done more than America to encourage and reward these professions; she also governs makers of toilet accessories, clothing manufacturers and dealers in articles of adornment —all of them activities in which America has attained front rank. Jupiter, the third of this heavenly trio, is the most powerful and the most American, because it gives honor, glory, wealth and the most sought-after thing in America, success.

Uranus, the planet which discards worn-out customs and forms of government, which breaks bonds and often causes estrangements, was also rising when our country was born, making July 4th, 1776, the predestined moment for us to shake off the yoke of monarchy and to set up in the New World a new form of government. Uranus has also had a marked effect on our later national life, for it is the planet which rules inventions in general and electrical inventions in particular, fields in which American genius has set a new pace for the world. But not all of Uranus' influence is good. It is, as I have already said, the heavenly planet which stirs revolutions and rebellion; and it is a fair assumption that whenever it completes its journey through the twelve signs and returns to the sign Gemini, ruling the United States—a cycle which takes eighty-four years—we may expect trouble of some sort. Uranus was in Gemini in 1776; and we rebelled against England. Exactly eighty-four years later, in 1860, Uranus was in Gemini again; and we had war between the North and the South. In 1942, Uranus again enters the sign Gemini— But I have said enough at this point to show you how the planets affect both character and destiny in their never-ending progression through the signs!

CONTENTS

PART ONE: ASTROLOGY—WHAT IT IS

THE SIGNS OF THE ZODIAC:

THE PLANETS:

CONTENTS

PART ONE

ASTROLOGY—WHAT IT IS

*"And God said, Let there be lights . . .
and let them be for signs and for seasons
and for days and years."*
—Genesis, I, 14.

*"And there shall be signs in sun and moon
and stars."*
—Gospel according
to St. Luke, XXI, 25.

THE SIGNS OF THE ZODIAC

"Heaven's golden alphabet—
And he that runs may read."
—YOUNG.

ARIES THE RAM

THE FIRST SIGN

"The Fire of God
Fills him. I never saw his like; there lives
No greater leader."
—TENNYSON.

ARIES

MARCH 22ND THROUGH APRIL 20TH *

ARIES, the first sign of the Zodiac, is the sign of leadership.

Aries is ruled—it it can be said that such a powerful and decided sign is ruled by *anything*—by the aggressive and warlike planet, Mars. There could hardly be a combination of influences more likely to produce a person of courage, initiative, ambition and force.

It *has* happened, in fact it too often does happen, that the Aries-born go down to defeat and destruction because these wonderful influences in their horoscopes become diverted into channels of a less constructive character. The finer the qualities, the more susceptible they seem to such perversion. Take the Aries characteristic and idealism. There is no finer quality within the gift of the starlit heavens. It has inspired leaders of men since the beginning of time. But if it is allowed to get the upper hand in the life of an Aries person, it converts enthusiasm into fanaticism, makes radicals out of liberals, causes otherwise sane people to "go off half-cocked."

On the other hand, this idealism of the typical native of Aries, if properly controlled, produces the most delightful companion, friend and lover. In the latter capacity, the Aries man shines in comparison with many of his brothers. There is nothing common or vulgar about his feelings for members of the opposite sex. He is ardent, demonstrative, even passionate; but always with admiration, usually with

---

* These dates vary slightly from year to year. If your birthday falls on the border-line between two signs, you should obtain from your astrologer accurate information on this point for your particular year.

worship, in his heart. And he must not be disturbed in this attitude. He must fancy himself the protector, the savior. He must be, as indeed he is, Sir Galahad, the Pure in Heart.

Aries women are no less idealistic than the Aries men. They, too, scorn the common and the vulgar. But in their relations with those they love, they are beset by dangers which are peculiar to them. Men in the rôle of saviors are not unattractive to the women they love. Women in the same rôle rather wear on the men they insist on saving. Men as leaders have always commanded the admiration of womankind. Women as leaders have been accepted rather recently and somewhat reluctantly by mankind!

In business, both sexes find a wonderful field for some of their best Aries qualities. The sign gives great executive ability, plus the personality necessary to carry authority in dealing with associates and subordinates. The Aries man or, for that matter, the Aries woman in business never says die. Industry is one of the prime qualities of this sign. And, as everybody with even the slightest business experience knows, the big prizes in the world of affairs go to those who are everlastingly "on the job."

The chief drawback to the success in business of the Aries-born—in fact, to their success in life—is the tendency to pay more attention to beginning things than to finishing them. There is something about their position at the head of the Zodiacal family—Gads, so to speak, of the whole human race—that bids them always to be starting something. This is a fine trait. It makes for activity, for interest, for progress—but, unless it is accompanied by a practicality and stick-to-it-iveness which is not always found in the natives of this sign, it does not make for accomplishment.

This tendency to scatter has an undermining effect not only on the work on which the Aries native is engaged but on the native himself. His naturally fine mentality is apt to become dissipated by a plethora of projects. His brain is likely to become like Stephen Leacock's Lochinvar, who mounted his horse and rode off in every direction. The best remedy for this tendency is thinking before acting. If the average Aries person would count ten before everything he did, he would be right ten times as often as he is when he acts on his first enthusiastic impulse. Introspection isn't good for most people; but a reasonable amount of it never hurt the Aries-born.

Aries, being the head sign of the Zodiac, the sign of people who get to the top, is naturally enough the head sign of the human body. It rules the top of the physical man just as it does the top of the spiritual one. Aries people should look out for injuries to the outside of their heads and to disorders of the inside. Sympathetically, Aries rules the stomach and the kidneys. Aries people should be careful of ailments that settle in those parts. Late in life, paralysis and apoplexy are menaces, against which the Aries-born must be on their guard. But, fortunately, the strength of Mars is the very thing which is required to protect its children against these ailments. Supplemented by reasonable living, especially as regards eating and drinking, the sturdy vitality of the Aries-Mars native should ensure a long and vigorous life.

According to Solar Biology, the sons and daughters of Aries find their most congenial mates among those born under either Leo or Sagittarius, and their least congenial ones among those born under Cancer, Libra, and Capricorn. But there is nothing final about these indications. It is true that the natives of the first two signs are naturally sympathetic and helpful to those born under Aries, and therefore should make excellent partners, either business or romantic. But each individual horoscope is so different from every other individual horoscope that there is no laying down rules on this point. The main thing is to find out all you can about your own characteristics as determined by the stars, and then do the same thing in regard to the characteristics of the "other person's."

As for yourself, remember that if you are a typical son or daughter of Aries, you have some of the faults of your virtues. Or you *may* have. Your courage may resolve itself into bravado; your daring into foolhardiness; your initiative into aggression; your strength into obstinacy; your ambition into lust for power; your idealism into lack of balance. But you mustn't let it! Remember also that Aries is symbolized by the Ram, famous both in mythology and in real life for its ability to get ahead. Its methods may not always be the gentlest. It may not yield easily or gracefully to direction or persuasion. But it "gets there"—even if it has to butt and horn and ram its way through those who stand in its path!

If You Were Born Between March 22nd and March 30th *—

You belong to the very first part of the very first sign of the Zodiac. You are by birth a pioneer, a leader of men —an adventurer in the best sense of that much abused word. And, thanks to the influence of your dominant planet, Mars, which not only rules the entire sign Aries but was especially powerful at the time you were born, you should possess the courage, energy and strength to fulfill your highest destiny.

If you are a true son or daughter of Mars, you are inclined to be aggressive almost to the point of antagonism. You should guard against this tendency, and do nothing to arouse the opposition of others. Strive for harmonious conditions in your office or in your home. These injunctions are very important to the Aries-born.

* All dates are inclusive.

You are distinctly the mental type. Your speech is witty, sometimes cynical. Your mind moves rapidly. You are impatient of routine. You do not care as much as you should for order. You have natural executive ability, but to get the best results, you should learn to plan your work before you work your plan.

Your planetary colors are scarlet, crimson, carmine, in fact, all reds; your natal flowers are the anemone, the hawthorn and the buttercup; your stones, the amethyst, the moonstone, the bloodstone and the diamond. If these colors, flowers and jewels do not become you, you do not need to wear them; but if you do, you will have the satisfaction of knowing that you are dressing in harmony with your stars.

Aries women are naturally very romantic. They are given to sudden enthusiasms. They are even violent in the expression of their affections, and do not create an atmosphere of rest, tranquillity, or serenity. You should remember these tendencies of the women of your sign, and try to cultivate some of the softer feminine qualities which are useful in holding the admiration which your brilliant nature is bound to attract.

If a man, you have a natural gift for political or public work. You would make an excellent military leader in time of war. In less troubled times, you should succeed in any sort of executive position connected with machinery. You ought to be a fine railroad man. Your pioneer nature makes you a wonderful starter of enterprises. See to it that you are a good finisher.

The planet Mars, which is doubly powerful in your horoscope, will undoubtedly have much to say about your choice of a profession. Mars favors especially soldiers, chemists, surgeons, barbers, workers in steel and iron, and mechanics generally. Its influence, however, is useful in any line requiring courage, aggressiveness, initiative, boldness and executive ability.

Physically, your stomach is not your strongest point; and neither are your kidneys. Avoid excessive use of sweets. Aries people are sometimes subject to paralysis and apoplexy late in life, but you should be able to avoid such ailments by reasonable diet and care. Be careful about injuries to your head and face.

Never forget the high possibilities of your sign. You can be a leader of your group, of your community, perhaps of your country. You can do a big work in the world. Do not miss these opportunities by being too aggressive and dictatorial. Do not cloud your vision with pettiness or conceit. Marshal the strength-giving forces of Mars, and fight the good fight. Fear nothing. The God of War is with you!

If You Were Born Between March 31st and April 9th—

You were never intended for a weakling. The Sun, "Giver of Life," and Mars, "God of War," were dominant in the heavens when you were born. And your astrological sign is Aries, symbolized by the Ram.

With this combination within you, you should be a most interesting person. You should be a leader in your community, either in private or public life. You should take a deep interest in political matters and sooner or later you will probably participate in them.

The Sun is the father of all the heavenly bodies. It gives honor, prestige, celebrity, position, power. Mars is also a powerful influence. It gives courage, energy, strength. The Sun makes its sons honest, truthful and noble. Mars makes its sons fearless, demonstrative and independent. With these good qualities may go some less desirable ones such as impulsiveness, cynicism, over-aggressiveness, easy anger. The degree of your success in life will depend on how well you use the good in your sign to conquer the less good.

Your physical dangers are chiefly connected with your stomach and kidneys. Watch your diet, especially sweets. Take plenty of exercise, guard against tendencies to apoplexy. Headaches, to which many Aries people are subject, are merely symptoms. Your general health should be good.

You possess great executive ability, but you have a tendency to scatter your forces. You begin things and do not always finish them. You are sometimes hasty in reaching conclusions, and even more hasty in acting on them. You need to order your thoughts, and your work, to be less impatient of routine. A reasonable amount of healthy introspection would do you no harm.

You are likely to succeed in any line of business which has to do with fire or machinery or in positions requiring social, political or military leadership.

Mars, the ruling planet of the sign Aries, governs most of these activities; also, surgeons, chemists, dentists, barbers, and workers in steel and iron. Less important, but still possibly influential in your choice of a profession, is the Sun, which rules jewelers, goldsmiths, and all those working with precious metals. The Sun also shines with especial favor on persons high in authority, on the leaders and rulers of men. In short, you have a wide field for your activities—and a most interesting one.

Your planetary colors are yellow, brown, and the blood-reds; your flowers, the anemone, the buttercup and the hawthorn; your stones, the diamond, the bloodstone, the amethyst and the chrysolite. If these colors, flowers and jewels do not become you, you do not need to wear them; but if you do, you will have the satisfaction of knowing that you are dressing in harmony with your stars.

If a woman, you must guard against being too dictatorial

in your relations with men. Forget that you are the pioneer, the leader—at least, appear to forget it. Men will be attracted to you by the brilliant rays of your favoring Sun. Don't let them be driven away by the over-aggressiveness of the war-like Mars.

Like most Aries people, men or women, you desire to rule. You must guard against arousing antagonism by a dictatorial manner. You must strive for harmonious relations with your associates. That way lies success!

If You Were Born Between April 10th and April 20th—

Venus, the Goddess of Love, and Mars, the God of War, were both dominant in the heavens when you entered this life, and they represent a very powerful array of planetary influences. Venus rules the particular part of the sign in which you were born. Mars rules the whole sign. As a result of this combination, you should have a loving nature —too impulsive, perhaps: too over-enthusiastic. You are fond of pleasure, of gaiety, of social amusements; but you have a place in your life for poetry and art.

Your disposition attracts friends. As a true child of Venus, you are naturally generous and kind. Your conversation is clever and sparkling. You should overcome the tendency to cynicism which is a characteristic of some people born in your sign. You are most attractive to the opposite sex.

The chief danger of your sign is too much aggressiveness; but the gentle influence of Venus should help you to avoid this peril. She will be of little help to you, however, in sticking to your task, once you have started it. Aries people are pioneers, great adventurers. They love to start things. They dislike the routine work of keeping things going. You must guard against the tendency to scatter the energies with which Mars has blessed you.

Do not forget that you were born under the first sign of the Zodiac, that you are a natural leader, and that you owe it to yourself to use this gift. Do not be swerved into unprofitable strife by the belligerent Mars or into unprofitable pleasure by the alluring Venus. Do not resent suggestions from others. Do not be petty or conceited or quarrelsome.

Your planetary colors are white, light blue, and all kinds of red; your flowers, the anemone, the hawthorn and the buttercup; your stones, the beryl, the green jasper, the coral, the carnelian, the amethyst, the sapphire and the diamond. If these colors, flowers and jewels do not become you, you do not need to wear them; but if you do, you will have the satisfaction of knowing that you are dressing in harmony with your stars.

Mars and Venus are both influential in your horoscope and since they both greatly influence the emotions, you should have an interesting life on the romantic side. In your case, Venus will soften the aggressive tendencies of Mars, and make you less aggressive in your attitude, less apt to insist on the Aries quality of leadership, less quarrelsome, less warlike than most Aries people. You should learn to cooperate in the family life, for if you do, you should make a brilliant success of your marriage.

The weak points of many Aries people are their stomachs and their kidneys. The ailments in later life to which they are most subject are paralysis and apoplexy. Fortunately, intelligent precautions begun early and followed consistently, especially as to diet and the avoidance of sweets, should ward off these perils and assure a long and healthy life.

Let the natural executive ability of your sign have full

play in some occupation congenial to you. Mars, the ruling planet of your sign and the most influential factor in your choice of a profession, favors soldiers, surgeons, chemists, dentists, barbers, and workers in iron and steel. Naturally, also, it rules the army and the navy.

On the other hand, the secondary influence wielded by Venus cannot be disregarded. Venus governs musicians, painters, poets, singers, actors, makers of toilet accessories, dealers in women's apparel, confectioners, perfumers and florists.

All Aries people tend to succeed in public life, in positions of political or military importance where leadership is essential to success, and in businesses connected with fire and machinery: for example, railways. But the Venus in your horoscope may lead you into more artistic pursuits. The main thing is: concentrate on whatever profession you choose —stick to it to the end!

TAURUS

THE SECOND SIGN

*"An honest man, close-buttoned
to the chin,
Broadcloth without, and a warm
heart within."*
—Cowper.

TAURUS

APRIL 21ST THROUGH MAY 21ST

TAURUS is the warm, friendly sign of the Zodiac. And
the typical Taurian is also warm, friendly, affectionate, passionate—but not demonstrative.

Every sign of the Zodiac has a symbol, which has been
given to it, not by chance, but out of the experience of the
ages. It is not for nothing that Taurus is symbolized by
the Bull. For the typical Taurian, glorying in his strength,
plunges and bellows through life to gain his goal.

And what a glorious strength it is, this strength of the
Bull! Taurians know what they want, and "they want what
they want when they want it." There is nothing namby-
pamby about this breed. Its strength is from the earth, and
it cares little how earthy it may seem to be.

But just as strong men are often the gentlest, this powerful sign makes those born under it peculiarly susceptible to
appeals to the softer side of their natures. In nothing does
this show more clearly than in the home life of the typical
native of Taurus. Taurus women are natural home-makers.
Taurus men, if they are true to their sign, are what the world
knows as "good providers." Both sexes glory in domesticity
to the exclusion of romance. They seem to care more for
their homes than they do for one another. And, by the same
token, they sometimes make more satisfactory parents than
they do husbands and wives.

I do not mean that the typical Taurian is not at heart
a loyal lover, for a dogged almost animalistic loyalty is often
a characteristic of the sign. But the inherent inability of

17

the Taurian native to express his affection in the day-to-day amenities of married life makes him or her a somewhat less engaging lover than the natives of many a less intensely sincere sign. With their children, however, this inhibition of the Taurians' seems to disappear—and, happily, some of the affection released by the presence of the child extends also to the parent. Taurians should always have children and they usually do.

Perhaps, I have stressed too much the side of the Taurian character symbolized by the Bull, and given too little emphasis to the side which expresses the softening and refining influence of Venus, the Goddess of Love and Beauty. For Venus, even when she finds herself in a matter-of-fact, feet-on-ground, middle-of-the-road sign like Taurus, is not to be denied.

Beauty is beauty, and in the Taurian nature, it finds expression, as one might expect, in the more utilitarian walks of life. The Taurian artist is not likely to concern himself with canvasses or with clay; he is much more apt to be the architect, the builder, the landscape-gardener, the interior decorator, the creator of communities in which man can live and work and fulfill his destiny.

The softer side of the Taurian nature may not find expression in poetic phrases, but it usually endows its possessor with a gentleness and a peacefulness and a serenity which makes him or her a most desirable companion in any relationship of life. The Taurian's feelings are not easily hurt, or if they are, the hurt does not find hasty, ill-timed expression. But do not rely too much, or too long, on the Taurian imperturbability. Once the native of this sign is convinced that he is being imposed upon, he rises in his might and becomes the Bull of Bashan himself in the expression of his passionate resentment.

In the physical man, Taurus rules the throat. That is the

reason why so many actors and actresses in the motion-picture world, who never reached the heights during the reign of the silent picture, suddenly came into their own with the advent of the talkies. They were either born strongly under the influence of Taurus or they were born with some important planet having to do with entertainment and the public —for example Venus, Neptune or the Moon—in the sign governing the throat. Many opera and concert singers are born strongly under this sign.

In the world of affairs, Taurians are not without qualifications for success. Venus, their Star of Destiny is known to astrologers as "The Lesser Fortune." This is not a deprecatory term. It is "lesser" only in comparison with the "greater fortune" bestowed by Jupiter. Both Jupiter and Venus— and Venus second only to Jupiter—stand for worldly success. In the case of those children of Venus who are born under the earthy sign Taurus, that success is most likely to come in those fields over which Taurus has special dominion. The Taurian is an earth child and out of the earth or under the earth he is most likely to find his fortune.

The strength of the Bull is an asset, too, in the struggle to reach the top. Once the typical Taurian has trained his mind's eye on a given goal, he is not likely to give up until he has attained it. He knows no fear; he seldom knows fatigue.

A very strong and very noble animal is the Bull!

If You Were Born Between April 21st and April 30th—

When you were born, the Sun was in the astrological sign Taurus, symbolized by the Bull. Venus is the ruling planet of that sign. You possess many of the finer qualities of the bull, because, like him, you are quiet and easy-going until aroused; inclined to do things your own way and to allow others to do the same. When aroused, however, you are inclined to be headstrong, unyielding, disregardful of consequences.

As a true child of Taurus, you have tremendous vitality, both physical and mental. You are exceedingly fond of comfort and luxury. But like most Taurian people you like to feel that your money has been wisely spent for matters connected with comfort in your home. You are especially fond of children. You are a loyal and devoted lover, but you fail sometimes to express your real affection.

Below your seeming imperturbability, you possess the ability to feel deeply; and since the part of the sign in which you were born is especially influenced by the intellectual planet Mercury, the combination of mind and heart is likely to produce a richly endowed nature.

The natural tendencies of people born in your sign are toward building, mining, farming, manufacturing, or some such practical pursuit. You, however, have two planets, Venus and Mercury, both prominent in your chart, and it may well be that their influence may divert you into less work-a-day professions.

Venus, which exerts the greater influence of the two because it is the ruling planet of the sign Taurus, favors artists, musicians, actors, makers of toilet accessories, manufacturers of women's clothing, confectioners, florists and all those who deal in articles of adornment.

Mercury, on the other hand, is the special god of literary men, booksellers, printers, teachers, accountants, interpreters, orators, registrars, clerks and letter carriers. So you see you have a wide field from which to choose. The main thing is to select some line which is congenial to you, and give to it the best that is in you.

Your planetary colors are lemon-yellow, red-orange, slate-color, pale blue and indigo; your flowers, the daisy, the cowslip, the syringa, the narcissus and the trailing arbutus; your stones, the emerald, the agate, the topaz, the marcasite, the lapis-lazuli, the coral and the beryl.   If these colors, flowers and jewels do not become you, you do not need to wear them; but if you do, you will have the satisfaction of knowing that you are dressing in harmony with your stars.

Taurus gives a warm, affectionate nature.   Venus gives the power to attract.   Do not let your persistence become a bar to your happiness.   And do not let your imperturbability keep you from showing the love that you feel.   In other words, let yourself go!

If You Were Born Between May 1st and May 9th—

Venus, Goddess of Love, and the Moon, ruler of the Senses, were prominent in the astrological heavens when you were born.

Your planetary colors are white, pale yellow, pale green, pale blue and lemon-yellow; your flowers, the violet, the lilac, the narcissus, the jonquil, the daisy, the cowslip and the crane's-bill; your stones, the opal, the moonstone, the carnelian, the coral, and all dull white and pale green jewels.   If these colors, flowers and jewels do not become you, you do not need to wear them; but if you do, you will have the satisfaction of knowing that you are dressing in harmony with your stars.

The sign of the Zodiac in which you were born is naturally an intensely practical sign.   Taurians tend to succeed in such pursuits as manufacturing, mining or building.   But you, with your Venus and Moon vibrations, may turn to less practical vocations.   You may do well as a journalist or public entertainer.   Or you may combine your practical and artistic tendencies in something like interior decorating.

With Venus the dominant planet of your sign, you should

have few difficulties in the field of love. The one thing you should guard against is the Taurian tendency to expect the "other person" to take your affection for granted. Tell him about it. Husbands like it—and so do wives!

Venus, the planet which will exert the greatest influence in your choice of a profession, favors musicians, painters, poets, actors and artists of all sorts. It also governs those engaged in the manufacture of women's clothing, makers of toilet accessories, florists, confectioners, perfumers, and dealers in articles of personal adornment.

The Moon, second only to Venus in its influence on your life calling, favors all those who "go down to the sea in ships." It governs transportation, especially by water; exporting and importing; and all businesses having to do with liquids. It is friendly to salesmen and others dealing with the general public.

Whatever line you take up, so long as it is congenial, you are likely to meet with ultimate success, because you possess the tenacity of the symbol of your sign, the Bull. You are a doer, not a dreamer. In fact, your mind is so filled with practical matters that you may forget at times to show the more appealing side of your nature.

Guard your naturally good health. Taurus people sometimes show a tendency toward laryngitis, tonsilitis and diphtheria, but if you live properly, keep your appetites in check, keep the pores open and the processes of elimination working, you should have little cause for worry.

You have an unusual equipment for success. Be sure that you use it properly. Develop a willingness to change your opinion—the Moon will help you to do that—when it can be shown that you are wrong. Don't be so tenacious in hanging on to what you have that you miss the opportunity which is just ahead of you. Don't go down with a sinking ship. You have the strength to swim—so swim!

If You Were Born Between May 10th and May 21st—

You were born under one of the strongest signs in the Zodiac, Taurus the Bull. Taurian people are blessed with tremendous vitality. They are practical, persistent, tenacious. Once they have started on a piece of work, nothing can deter them from finishing it. All of these traits, when properly understood and controlled, make for success.

You have the warm, affectionate Taurus nature and the Venus charm to attract and hold members of the opposite sex. You should guard against a failure to express the feelings which you have in your heart. Show your appreciation of your lover's good qualities. Let him or her know that you care.

Taurus makes for a happy domestic life and if you are a true son or daughter of Taurus, you appreciate above most things in life the peace and comfort of a good home. You are good-tempered and agreeable so long as you are not goaded into action. Then look out! Taurians are haters as well as lovers. They must be careful not to let themselves go too far in either direction.

You must not let the more depressing influences of Saturn, the planet which rules over the part of the sign Taurus in which you were born, control your life. He is a strict disciplinarian.

Your physical strength should be an asset, too. Do nothing to dissipate it. Curb your appetite. Live for the mental and the spiritual rather than the physical. Keep active all of the natural functions of your body. Give special care to the throat.

In business or in the home, if you throw off the depression which may sometimes possess you, there should be no doubt of your ultimate success. If a man, you have special gifts for practical, constructive work: mining, manufacturing, building and farming. Saturn's influence is all on the side of such practical endeavors. It may even lead you into lines of work which are far more solemn: many sextons, undertakers and grave-diggers are born under Saturn!

However, Saturn's influence, strong as it is, does not constitute the dominant power in your chart. Venus, the goddess of love and beauty, is the ruling planet of your sign, and as such will very likely divert you into lighter and perhaps more inspiring professions. Venus governs musicians, painters, poets, actors, artists of all kinds; it also rules makers of toilet accessories, manufacturers of women's clothing, dealers in articles of ornamentation and good things to eat. So you see you have a wide field from which to choose your highway to success.

Your planetary colors are pale blue, indigo, lemon-yellow, black, dark brown and lead-gray; your flowers, the trailing arbutus, the violet, the hyacinth, the daisy, the cowslip and the jonquil; your stones, the lodestone, the moonstone, the opal, the beryl, the carnelian, the sapphire and the chrysolite. If these colors, flowers, and jewels do not become you, you do not need to wear them; but if you do, you will have the satisfaction of knowing that you are dressing in harmony with your stars.

Remember that you belong to one of the staunchest signs in the whole Zodiac; that you are under the influence of the most charming of all planets, Venus; that you are endowed by Saturn with the power to realize your highest ideals through industry on the material plane; and that you have within you, as your own astrological right, the strength of the Bull, the symbol of your sign!

GEMINI

THE THIRD SIGN

"Variety is the mother of Enjoyment."
　　　　　—Disraeli.

GEMINI

"So like they were, no mortal
Might one from other know;
White as snow their armor was,
Their steeds were white as snow."
—MACAULAY'S LAYS OF ANCIENT ROME.

THERE is no subject in literature or in life more intriguing, more baffling than this one of twins. From these fabled sons of Jupiter and Leda down to the latest amazing, and doubtless surprising, double addition to the neighbour's family, the world has been agog over this often-recurring but never fully explained manifestation of Mother Nature. Why are they alike? Why are they different? And no one can tell who doesn't read the answer in the stars.

So it is in astrology. There is no more interesting and no more elusive problem for the astrologer than is presented by the complex nature of the children of Gemini, that sign of the Zodiac which is symbolized in astrological lore by the figures of the Twins. The natives of Aries may be more idealistic; the natives of Taurus may be more dependable; but the sons and daughters of Gemini are the perpetual question marks of the Zodiacal family.

As you know, I am not given to indulgence in technical astrological language, but there could hardly be three better representatives of traditional groupings in the astrological family than the sign Aries, which belongs to the fire triplicity; and the sign Taurus, which belongs to the earth triplicity; and the sign Gemini, which belongs to the air triplicity.

Aries people *are* fiery, Taurus people *are* earthy and Gemini people *are* airy! And there is a reason for their airiness, apart from the traditional grouping to which they have been assigned. For Gemini is ruled by the planet Mercury, the Winged Messenger of the Gods, from whom we have acquired the adjective "mercurial." Gemini people go up and down like the mercury in the thermometer. They are light as air —and, alas, sometimes as changeable! For the extraordinary immobility of the Gemini character is not confined to "up" and "down." The average Gemini native goes backward and forward, right and left, up and down, with equal facility.

I wouldn't have you think that the influence of Mercury is a bad influence. How could it be, since it rules the intellect and imparts to those born under it the high mental qualities for which it stands? But even Mercury, with all its power, is not above being influenced—and the influence of the Twins, especially in those moments when they are pulling in opposite directions, is strong. The first duty of the native of Gemini, therefore, is to mobilize the intellectual strength, which is his heritage, and prevent it from being dissipated by the disorganizing elements in the sign under which he was born.

Mercury in Gemini gives versatility, volatility, facility; it gives suavity, tactfulness, diplomacy; it gives understanding, intuition, vision. These are high qualities. They should be used by the Gemini-born to further aims, to achieve great ends. The Gemini native's chief problem is himself. He must recognise his dual possibilities. Realising the difficulty which he will have in concentrating on any one line of effort, he must give himself more than one thing to do. If he has a vocation, which exercises one set of mental muscles, he must choose an avocation, which exercises another set. He must keep both of his twins busy. But if he is wise he will choose for them activities which lead by varying routes to the same goal.

If he is a man he will adopt a profession or a business in which quickness of mind and extreme mental facility are the chief requirements for success; and during business hours, he will use all of the strength of character which he possesses to the furtherance of the work on which he is engaged. After business hours, he will turn his active mind to some artistic or literary pursuit, quite different perhaps from the interest which has filled his day, but which in some way improves his equipment for his daily task.

If the Gemini subject is a woman, she will contrive to make her high mental gifts take the place of natural aptitude in the performance of her domestic duties. Gemini women are not natural house-wives but they usually possess the ability and adaptability essential to success in planning or running a home. This task performed, and for the Gemini woman it is a task—she can then satisfy her longing for a more strictly intellectual career in some activity which will make her a more interesting companion or a more successful mate.

I stress this double-barrelled life, because I believe it is essential to the welfare and happiness of the Gemini-born. They are all too apt to scatter their forces, anyhow; and I believe it is for their good, as well as for the good of all those who are associated with them or dependent on them, that they should do their mental dissipating according to a well-thought-out plan. But the possibility of working off their excess brain energy in such a manner does not relieve the children of Gemini from the responsibility of overcoming, so far as possible, the besetting sin of their sign: the failure to concentrate.

No one can do things more easily than the Gemini-born.

No one can do things more gracefully. No one can do them more successfully—if only they will do them at all! But that driving force which makes the son of Aries scale the heights, and that wholesome sense of responsibility and obligation which makes the son of Taurus plod on, feet-on-the-ground, to attain his goal, are lacking in the make-up of the natives of the third sign. They must recognise this lack and they must substitute for it a deliberate determination to do their job and to stick to it to the end.

It is not only in business that the son of Gemini sometimes fails to concentrate; it is equally true of his activities in the world of romance. Gemini husbands are often flirts, sometimes philanderers, and because of their tendency to scatter their attentions, they frequently lose the affection of the persons whom they really love. In the same way, Gemini wives, who are at heart faithful to their husbands, land in the divorce courts because they cannot resist the temptation to have too many irons in the fires of romance.

But these faults of the Gemini-born are largely on the surface. They are the sins of superficiality. They should not be allowed—and they *will* not be allowed by the stronger members of this astrological family—to obscure the high mental gifts which are their Zodiacal birthright. Mercury, the God of Intellect is with them—and he is a powerful ally!

If You Were Born Between May 22nd and May 31st—

You were born under Gemini, the astrological sign which rules the United States, and you possess that trait which is most characteristic of the American people: versatility.

As a true son or daughter of Gemini, this is your strength and your weakness.

The planet Mercury, which rules the intellect, is the dominant planet of your sign. You have, therefore, a highly developed, extremely sensitive mentality. You see both sides of every subject. You must cultivate decision, and not be swerved too easily by the opinion of others.

Gemini is symbolized by the Twins—and from this fact you may take a hint as to one way to cure your tendency to scatter. Resolve yourself into two persons by carrying along two kinds of work at the same time. When you are tired of one, turn to the other. This will satisfy your desire for change, and will at the same time keep you from wandering off the road of accomplishment. If both activities contribute to a common end, so much the better. But the two-job idea, even if one is merely a fad or an avocation, is almost essential to the Gemini person's success.

An excellent memory and an insatiable curiosity are two of your most marked mental characteristics. Use these gifts wisely. Concentrate on the matter in hand; cultivate will-power; and learn to stand on your own feet.

Be especially careful of your nerves. Cultivate calm, mentally and physically. Get plenty of exercise in the open air. Get more sleep than most people need. Live so as to avoid neuritis and rheumatic difficulties affecting the nerve centers.

Jupiter was dominant in that part of the sign Gemini in which you were born. Your generous disposition, your humane impulses, and your ability to rise to great heights come from the influence of that beneficent planet. If you are a true son or daughter of Jupiter, you may also possess unusual oratorical powers and a taste for judicial, literary or artistic pursuits.

Mercury, which is the dominant planet of your sign, is especially favorable to people connected with the production of literature: writers, editors, publishers, printers and booksellers. It also favors teachers, accountants, interpreters, registrars and clerks.

Jupiter, on the other hand, plays few favorites. It may

seem to be especially fond of lawyers, bankers, clergymen, doctors, judges, people in high places, but it exerts its beneficent influence on all lines of endeavor. You are especially fortunate in having Jupiter with you—whatever line you may choose.

Your planetary colors are orange, yellow, slate-color, purple and violet; your flowers, the lily of the valley, the myrtle, the Mayflower, and the bittersweet; your stones, the beryl, the emerald, the sapphire, the agate, the topaz and the marcasite. If these colors, flowers and jewels do not become you, you do not need to wear them; but if you do, you will have the satisfaction of knowing that you are dressing in harmony with your stars.

Gemini people are facile in love as in all other matters. They love beauty in their surroundings, and believe in "atmosphere." The home of a Gemini woman is above all charming. If she can keep from having too many irons in the fire—flirtatious irons, I mean—she should make a most successful wife!

If You Were Born Between June 1st and June 9th—

When you were born, the Sun was in the astrological sign Gemini, symbolized by the Twins. Mercury, which rules the intellectual life, also rules this sign.

The result of this combination is sure to be a highly sensitive, many-sided mentality capable of high achievements and subject to deep pitfalls. Most Gemini people are ravenous in their hunger for knowledge, and versatile in their schemes for applying it. But they get more pleasure out of the doing than out of the achieving. They often have the work and somebody else has the results.

Your own situation is complicated by the fact that Mars was also dominant in the heavens at the time you were born

Mars gives his children strength, courage, boundless energy, traits which make for success. But Mars also gives a tendency toward over-aggressiveness, quarrelsomeness, and violence. Don't let these latter traits dominate your character.

The Gemini "cure-all," especially for a person with your strong Mars influence, is concentration. Stick to the matter in hand, or the matters. You may have to carry along two interests in order to keep your mind occupied and to satisfy your desire for change. If you do, try to make both work to one end.

Your planetary colors are blood-red, green, blue, yellow, slate-color and scarlet; your flowers, the myrtle, the bitter-sweet, the lily of the valley and the Mayflower; your stones, the moon crystal, the beryl, the agate, the emerald and the topaz. If these colors, flowers and jewels do not become you, you do not need to wear them; but if you do, you will have the satisfaction of knowing that you are dressing in harmony with your stars.

You will be successful with members of the opposite sex if you don't try to pick fights with them. Mars is inclined to make its children a bit contentious. Don't give yourself up to petty strife. Use the Mars influence to strengthen your character and your charm. Don't try to do too many things at one time. Concentrate on the person you love. Remember that though Gemini may be symbolized by the Twins, you are just one individual.

Natives of Gemini are usually high-strung. Their nerves give way first. Rest yours all you can. Take plenty of exercise. Breathe plenty of fresh air. Eat conservatively. Cultivate physical and mental poise.

Men born in your sign make excellent lawyers, bankers, and diplomats. They are effective public speakers. If they can command themselves, they can command the world.

Mercury, ruling your sign and also ruling the intellect,

will be of service to you in any line you adopt for your life
work. It is especially favorable to writers, editors, publishers,
printers, booksellers; also to teachers, accountants, orators,
registrars and clerks.

Mars, second only to Mercury in its influence on your
choice of a profession, favors soldiers, surgeons, chemists,
dentists, barbers, dealers in steel and iron and all workers
with sharp instruments. Its influence will help you, however, in almost any position requiring courage, initiative,
aggressiveness and executive ability.

Avoid discussions. Gemini people never gain their points
by argument and strife. Exert your charm. Avoid restlessness, too, stick on the job. And do it!

If You Were Born Between June 10th and June 21st—

You were born in the airy, intellectual sign Gemini, and
in many ways you are among the most fortunate of the natives of this sign. The Sun, which rules honor, fame and
advancement in life, was dominant in the heavens when you
were born.

Your planetary colors are yellow-brown, orange, slate-color
and gold; your flowers, the Mayflower, the myrtle, the bitter-
sweet, and the lily of the valley; your stones, the chrysolite,
the beryl, the emerald and the topaz. If these colors, flowers
and jewels do not become you, you do not need to wear them;
but if you do, you will have the satisfaction of knowing that
you are dressing in harmony with your stars.

Men born under Gemini tend to succeed as brokers, bankers, lawyers and diplomats. Their oratorical powers make
them effective in public life. You should do well in any of
these lines which appeal to you, but, with your sun ruling
the part of the sign in which you were born and with Mer-

cury ruling the whole sign, you might find your greatest happiness in literature, science or art.

The Sun looks with special favor on public officials and on all those in high places. It has a special care for jewelers and those who work in precious metals. Mercury, on the other hand, which is the ruling planet of your sign and the chief factor in determining your choice of a profession, favors all those engaged in the production of literature: writers, printers, publishers, editors and booksellers; also accountants, interpreters, teachers and clerks.

You may not choose any of these professions for your own, but whatever line you follow, you will have with you the beneficent influence of your two dominant planets: the Sun giving strength and Mercury giving brain-power.

The symbol of your sign is significantly the Twins. And you possess the characteristic versatility of your sign. Do not let it degenerate into changeableness.

Extreme versatility, a highly developed mentality, and an over-sensitive nature are usually accompanied by an over-supply of nerves. Gemini people are generously equipped with these necessary but discomforting telephone connections between the body and the brain. Do not strain the wires. If you do you may suffer from neuritis and rheumatic pains in the arms, shoulders and nerve centers. Diet, exercise and fresh air are the preventive measures you should adopt. And, if you do, there is every chance of your realizing the high possibilities of your sign.

You may not acquire great fortune in the material sense. The result of work is never so important to a native of Gemini as the work itself. You may even pass through periods of anxiety and restlessness. And you may go on many journeys before you sail into safe harbor. But if you steer your course carefully, success will eventually be yours. Perhaps more than success—perhaps fame!

CANCER

THE FOURTH SIGN

"Diana's foresters, gentlemen of the shade, minions of the moon."
—SHAKESPEARE.

CANCER

Now we come to the fourth sign—and the fourth *kind* of sign—in the Zodiac. Aries was fire; Taurus, earth; Gemini, air; now Cancer is water—symbolized by the Crab and ruled by the Moon.

That doesn't mean that there is anything wishy-washy about Cancer people. Crabs aren't wishy-washy, once they get their hold on anything or anybody; and neither are those human beings who are born between the 22nd of June and the 23rd of July. In fact, if there is one quality more than another that stands out in the natives of this sign, it is tenacity.

The love of the Cancer-born, once it is fixed, grows into an enduring loyalty which belies the watery nature of their sign and defies the influence of the ever-changing Moon. And that love extends to much more than the single person who inspires it; it embraces the home, the family, the neighborhood and the community in which the Cancer person lives. It goes back into the past and enshrines traditions and precedents and customs and habits. It claims its own, and it sticks to it to the end.

But not without a fight! For the influence of the Moon, the fastest moving of all planets, is all on the side of travel and adventure, of voyages to foreign lands, of search for new landscapes and new seascapes—especially seascapes.

Cancer people cannot deny this influence. It is always there, urging them to abandon the home of their fathers. They make great sailors, sea captains, explorers; at least, some of them do. But the typical Cancerite, after years of struggling with the wanderlust, comes back to the place where he was born. There he is happiest. There, nine times out of ten, he will live and die. For it was undoubtedly of a Cancer type that the poet wrote:

"Land of my Sires! What mortal hand
Can e'er untie the filial band
That knits me to thy rugged strand."

But this conflict which is forever going on in the minds and hearts of the Cancer-born is not without effect on their methods of thought and action. The typical native of Cancer is a moody soul. If he is highly developed, he is master of his moods; if not, he is their slave.

There is a feminine sensitiveness about even the most masculine Cancer person which is directly traceable to the influence of the feminine deity that rules the sign. This sensitiveness, which is almost as universal a Cancer trait as tenacity, can be developed into a fine adaptability, which enables its possessor to get the best out of the life around him and to give to that life the best that is in him; or it may drive him into himself, submit him to the tortures of introspection and self-analysis, and make him a hermit even in the house of his friends.

The first of these alternatives is, of course, the one for which the natives of this sign should strive; and if they succeed in attaining it, they may become inspiring influences in the great world. Many successful preachers, inspiring teachers and eloquent orators are Cancer-born.

Obviously, the sensitiveness of Cancer people is a factor to be dealt with by their associates as well as by themselves. Coercion of any kind invariably engenders resentment in their hearts. It is essential that parents, teachers—yes, and husbands and wives!—of the Cancer-born should treat them with understanding sympathy.

In love there is no one more romantic or imaginative than sons and daughters of the Moon. They are born for love, these sensitive, loyal Cancer people; and they glory in its nuances. But they are often too proud to display their feelings to others. They are naturally shy; they fear ridicule; they dread the possibility of repulse. Because of these traits, they frequently stumble into long series of misunderstandings with those they love, and find themselves at the end in the presence of a disaster which they do not deserve and of whose causes they are only in the vaguest way aware.

More often than not, however, their own patience and tenacity in the face of troubles which would discourage a less enduring affection, saves them from themselves. Sooner or later, they break down the barriers—often self-imposed—which stand between them and the object of their affections; and then, if that object is worthy, there ensues a lasting and wholly satisfying relationship.

There is a good deal of the prophet about the higher type of Cancer person. It has often been said that the past and the future are as clear to him as the present. It is certainly true of the past. In fact, one of his gravest dangers is living too much in the past. But the extreme sensitiveness of the Cancer temperament makes its possessor also peculiarly susceptible to impressions about events still to come. Their vision of the future, however, is usually an outgrowth of their study of the past. The Cancer prophet is seldom of revolution, but rather of reform. He beckons to well-established heights, not to uncharted ones. And he is slow to take the direct path up the hill; he prefers to move side-wise like the Crab.

In the physical man, Cancer rules the stomach; and this fact has an important bearing on the whole Cancer nature.

New York City was born under Cancer, and that is why it is one of the diningest-out cities in the world. Cancer brides often spend so much money on their dining room furniture that they have nothing left with which to furnish the rest of the house. Cancer husbands sometimes become so interested in the affairs of the family kitchen that they make nuisances of themselves around the house. And Cancer people of all sorts and kinds have a tendency to exaggerate the importance eating plays in the scheme of human happiness. Cancer, being a watery sign and ruled by that watery luminary, the Moon, also has dominion over liquids—and the Cancer-born should always recognize the fact that drinking as well as eating may become a menace to their health and to their success.

The chief cause for worry, however, in the horoscope of the average Cancer person is worry, itself. Most of the physical troubles which assail the natives of this sign come from mental or emotional causes. Cancer people fret and worry over the people they love until they make themselves ill; then they fret and worry over themselves. It is a vicious circle; and Cancer people should take precautions against starting on its weary round. It may be that they are not the sturdiest members of the Zodiacal family. The Moon is not so strong as the Sun, or as robust as Jupiter, or as vigorous as Mars. But Cancer people are not weaklings. If they can control their minds, they can control their bodies—at least, they can with the help of reasonable diet and physical care.

Fortunately, the Cancer-born have within themselves the very quality to help them overcome any tendency they may have toward fretfulness, touchiness, even bitterness—and that is patience. Cancer suffers much, and endures much. Like its symbol, the Crab, it never lets go!

If You Were Born Between June 22nd and July 1st—

Venus and the Moon dominate your life. The moon governs the home, the mother, the public generally; your place of birth and of residence: your voyages, your worldly position and your marital affairs.

Venus governs love and art. It is a principal factor in your enjoyment of social pleasures. It has to do with your jewels, your clothes and, to some extent, your money.

The influence of these two dominant bodies in your astrological chart is modified by the conservative sign Cancer, appropriately symbolized by the Crab. The result is a somewhat paradoxical combination of traits productive of interesting but complex personalities.

Your planetary colors are light blue, violet, silver, white, lemon-yellow, pale green and pale blue; your flowers, the moon flower, and the wallflower (no insult intended); your stones, the opal, the moonstone, the crystal and all dull white or pale green jewels. If these colors, flowers and jewels do not become you, you do not need to wear them; but if you do, you will have the satisfaction of knowing that you are dressing in harmony with your stars.

Toward those you love you are affectionate and protective. You have little of the coquetry of the Gemini or the flirtatiousness of the daughter of Libra. Yours is a chaste, constant love. You like good things to eat yourself and you know how to provide them for others. In short, you know that the way to a man's heart is still through his stomach!

Superficially, you are apt to be changeable and restless, but underneath there is a praiseworthy tenacity of purpose which should be cultivated. Your normal attitude toward those you love is affectionate and protective. You can even be self-sacrificing and long-suffering.

You have a strong sentiment for the past; you treasure

heirlooms and esteem pedigrees. You combine a love of tranquil domesticity with a desire for frequent travel, a craving for new sensations and adventures, especially on the sea.

If a man, the latter trait may lead you into shipping enterprises, importing and exporting, or other business ventures having to do with water. All Cancer natives also have a natural gift for chemistry, and for any activity connected with food.

Venus, one of your two dominant planets, favors confectioners, bakers, and pastry cooks; also makers of toilet accessories, manufacturers of women's clothing and dealers in articles of personal adornment. Venus is also the goddess of musicians, poets, painters, actors, artists generally. If you have talent along any of these lines, you should develop it. Venus will help you to succeed with it.

The Moon, which is even more influential in your choice of a profession because it is the ruling planet of your sign, governs sailors, shipping merchants, dealers in liquids, exporters and importers, travelers and all those engaged in transportation, especially by water. So you see you have a wide field from which to choose.

Don't let your love of liquids lead to over-indulgence in the alcoholic kind. Guard against gastric disturbances and weak digestion. Be careful of your throat. Simple living is your best remedy—and your best preventive!

If You Were Born Between July 2nd and July 11th—

Cancer, the astrological sign under which you were born, is symbolized by the Crab. But it is far more agreeable in its influence than either its name or its symbol would indicate.

Men and women born under Cancer often rise to positions of great prominence. Cecil Rhodes who ruled South Africa with an iron hand, Lord Northcliffe who became the most influential man in the British Empire, Calvin Coolidge who became President of the United States, and John D. Rockefeller who became the richest man in the world were all Cancer people. A sign of the Zodiac which can produce such men as these is worthy of profound respect.

You are not only fortunate in being born in this sign but you are fortunate in being a native of a most favoring part of it—the part which is ruled by the intellectual planet Mercury. With such a combination, you should win fame or fortune.

You may be accused of fickleness, but it is not a fair accusation. You are capable of great self-sacrifices for the person you love. You are thin-skinned, highly sensitive, and suffer from fancied slights. But you are conspicuously loyal. There is a singleness of purpose about the Cancer woman's love which sets her above all her sisters. She loves one man 'til she dies. A Cancer man also loves romance, but he loves domesticity more. His attitude toward the woman he loves is protective and paternal rather than amorous.

Your planetary colors are white, pale yellow, pale green, violet, silver, blue and black; your flowers, the wallflower (no insult intended!) and the moon flower; your stones, the marcasite, the agate, the topaz, the emerald, the opal, the moonstone and the crystal. If these colors, flowers and jewels do not become you, you do not need to wear them; but if you do, you will have the satisfaction of knowing that you are dressing in harmony with your stars.

Avoid over-eating, excessive use of alcohol and self-indulgence of all sorts. Guard against asthma. Avoid over-straining the vocal cords.

The Moon, which is the ruler of your sign and hence a

most important factor in determining your profession, favors all who deal in liquids or "go down to the sea in ships." It governs sailors, shipping merchants, travelers, fishermen, those engaged in transportation, especially by water.

Mercury, on the other hand, favors those engaged in the production of literature: printers, publishers, editors, booksellers and writers: it also favors accountants, clerks, salesmen, teachers, interpreters and letter carriers. So you see you have a wide field from which to choose your life work.

In whatever line you choose you should guard against oversensitiveness. It is likely to make enemies out of acquaintances and business associates and to cause temporary discord and embarrassment among your friends. Harmony is essential to your fullest development.

Cultivate confidence in yourself. Dare to defy tradition. Don't say, "What was good enough for my father is good enough for me." Perhaps it isn't!

If You Were Born Between July 12th and July 23rd—

Cancer, the astrological sign under which you were born, rules the city of New York. And its natives, like the natives of New York, seem bent on running the gamut of human experience.

The Moon, which is the ruler of this sign, was especially influential at the time you were born, so you are probably a lover of travel, adventure, and the occult. You will doubtless undergo many changing conditions in your life. You may gain public recognition and you may acquire property without especially aiming to do so.

However, if you possess the conservatism of your sign as symbolized by the Crab, you will hold fast to traditions and will hesitate to cut yourself off from familiar surroundings.

I cannot tell which course you will finally adopt. That depends largely on aspects in your individual horoscope. In
the case of most Cancer people, however, the conservative
element finally conquers.

Your planetary colors are violet, pale yellow, pale green,
silver and white; your flowers, the moon flower and the wallflower (no insult intended!); your stones, the moonstone,
the crystal, the opal, the dull white and pale green gems. If
these colors, flowers and jewels do not become you, you do
not need to wear them; but if you do, you will have the
satisfaction of knowing that you are dressing in harmony
with your stars.

Your clinging to the traditions of those who have gone
before you is a fine thing sentimentally; but practically it
is apt to be an obstacle to your success. It tends to increase
that lack of self-confidence, which is one of the few conspicuous failings of the Cancer-born subject. You must
acquire self-confidence somehow if you are to fulfill your
greatest destiny.

You are very dependent on your friends, and you must
not alienate them by taking offence at fancied slights. Do
not confuse your vision of the future with memories of the
past. And do not allow yourself to be hyper-sensitive.

Your interest in travel might lead you very naturally into
such pursuits as shipping and importing and exporting.
Your interest in good things to eat might turn you toward
dietetics and chemistry. Your love of children would help
to bring you success in any activity connected with the care
of the young.

The Moon, which is the dominant planet in your chart,
governs sailors, shipping merchants, importers and dealers in
liquids of all sorts, and also favors salesmen and others dealing with the public. You can hardly go wrong if you find
yourself following any of these varied professions.

On the physical side, you should be on guard against asthma, throat trouble, gastric difficulties, and chronic indigestion. But if you live simply, keeping your appetite in check and satisfying your thirst with water rather than alcohol, you should live to a happy old age!

LEO

THE FIFTH SIGN

"Although too much of a soldier among sovereigns, no one could claim with better right to be a sovereign among soldiers."
—Sir Walter Scott.

LEO

JULY 24TH THROUGH AUGUST 23RD

THE royal sign—that's what Leo is. Napoleon was born under it! So was Mussolini! And so was George Bernard Shaw!

If you are a typical son or daughter of Leo, you, too, are the masterful, high-minded type, possessing great executive ability. You may exercise this ability in either business or social life. Leo people are kings of the circle to which they belong. They were born to rule and they see to it that they do so. It is essential that they keep their desire for authority within reasonable bounds. Otherwise, they may become arrogant and domineering.

Leo people have magnetic personalities. They should always see in person those whom they wish to influence. They also have a natural dislike for anything petty or underhanded. They are ambitious, industrious, untiring, but they dislike menial tasks. They should not let their ambition make them unhappy or discontented. A wholesome amount of discontent won't do them any harm, but they must not let it rule their lives. Leo people derive a great deal of their strength from the Sun, which is the dominating heavenly body of this powerful sign. And since the Sun governs certain parts of the human body—notably the heart, the back and the arteries—those of you who were born in the last weeks of July and the first three weeks of August should look out for symptoms of trouble in those parts. The Sun's ailments are organic rather than functional, so take warning if you suffer from faintings, weak eyesight, palpitations of the heart or any other disorders of the arterial system.

The natives of this sign are natural executives. If they
can't be at the head of the business in which they are engaged—and not everybody can—they should be connected if
possible with the executive branch. They make excellent
superintendents, managers, sales managers, directors or officers
of corporations—in fact, they fit acceptably any position in
which they can be the "boss."

Fortunately, they are inclined to use their gifts for the
common good. They are naturally high-minded. They possess a well-developed sense of noblesse oblige. They are invariably generous. They are untiring workers. They possess
rare executive ability. They deserve to be kings!

There are feminine lions in this world, too; and feminine
royalties. It is significant that Ethel Barrymore, head of
the royal family of Broadway and acknowledged queen of
the American stage, was born strongly under Leo! The Leo
wife wishes to dominate, just as the Leo husband does. And
her personality is so magnetic that she usually succeeds. Her
husband, if he is wise, will accept this fact philosophically,
and will content himself with encouraging her to work off
her leonine energies in "good works." If he does, his reward
will be great: for love is the real kingdom of the Leo woman.

People born under the fiery sign Aries or the frank, open
sign Sagittarius are generally considered the most appropriate
mates for Leo people. Certainly, according to the position
of the Sun in their horoscopes, they should prove most congenial. But before deciding such a personal matter as matrimony, the scientific astrologer must insist on knowing not
only the month of your birth but the year and the day, and,
if possible, the hour and the place. And then, it isn't possible to foretell the result of the marriage unless the same information is available about "the other person." The great
thing in marriage is to have the two charts harmonize. Then,

the people will harmonize. Then, and then only, success and happiness will wait upon love.

One trouble with Leo people—whether they are in love or not!—is that they want to rule in *everything*. They should not try to be the dominating force all the time. Their magnetic personalities and inherent abilities will attract the big things to them, anyway. They should let other people have their way in the non-essentials. Their energies are too valuable to dissipate them on efforts which other people can manage just as well.

Another danger which Leo people face is the temptation to show off. Leo people are "good," and they know it. So does everybody else. They don't need to impress others with their ability. It sticks out all over them. And they should be sparing also with their authority. He who has the greatest authority seldom shows it. At all times, they should keep in subjection their natural love of praise. They should remember the words of the poet:

> " 'Tis an old maxim in the schools
>   That flattery's the food of fools."

When annoyed or angered, the Leo-born retaliate openly because they despise anything petty or underhanded. They frequently gain their own way by sheer force of personal charm and pleasing manner. They should find this trait a valuable asset in their dealings with the business and social world. Leo people do not have many difficulties because of lack of personal magnetism. In fact, they are likely to invite envy or jealousy because of their friends and admirers. But they have little patience with "red tape." It is not easy for them to realise that big enterprises move slowly. They must be willing to progress step by step, if they hope to reach their goal.

I emphasise these dangers of your sign because it is imperative that you avoid them in order to fulfill your obvious destiny. For it is inconceivable from an astrologer's standpoint that you should not be a strong, forceful person, aspiring to command and capable of exercising it. You should be keen for adventure and hazardous undertakings. You should succeed at home and in foreign countries.

In fact, you may well tremble lest you fail to make a wise and complete use of the great gifts with which the stars have showered you!

If You Were Born Between July 24th and August 2nd—

You were born in Leo, the royal sign of the Zodiac. The Sun, Giver of Life, rules this sign, and its symbol is the Lion.

Leo is the only sign ruled by the Sun. It emanates vibrations which play upon that which is within, back of and beyond the brain consciousness. Leo people have the traits of the Lion, which, though often gentle and kindly, is inherently masterful. Those born under this sign are impetuous and impulsive and when their affections are involved, sometimes passionate. Constancy and loyalty are two of their characteristic traits.

The Leo-born are naturally intuitive. But it is most necessary that they be careful to distinguish between intuition and mere impulse. They should never reply hastily to an unpleasant letter or make an important decision without calm reflection. On the other hand, they must not allow their judgment to force them to go contrary to their intuitions in regard to people with whom they have dealings. Their determined will and self-confidence may, at times, cause them to take an attitude which will appear to be boastful, too dictatorial, and over-ambitious.

People endowed with such strong qualities usually need

strict discipline, and the stars have seen to it that you get yours from the greatest of all disciplinarians, the planet Saturn, which was also dominant in the heavens at the time you were born. With Saturn so influential in your horoscope, you must guard against self-deception, false pride, domestic infelicity and hazardous speculations. Cultivate a wise self-confidence. Do not assert yourself at the wrong moment.

Take care of your health. The ailments from which you are most likely to suffer, are those which have to do with the heart and back. Avoid violent fits of temper and physical over-exertion. Live sensibly. These simple precautions, combined with the great vitality which belongs to Leo's children, should ward off disease of all sorts and assure you a long and healthy life.

Leo rules not only the physical heart, but also the love nature. It is, therefore, most necessary that you have a normal outlet for your emotions, as you are very dependent on affection. In fact, your desire for praise and approval may tend to become an exaggerated ego, or "exhibition complex." It would be well for you to remember the old adage that "he who has the greatest authority seldom shows it." You should avoid giving way to "fits" of temper, and over-exertion, because of the ill effects it may have on the heart. You should try and rise above any sorrow you may have, for if you nurse it, it will have a very disorganizing effect on your health.

If you are a woman, and wish to be attractive to men, don't forget that the besetting sin of the daughters of Leo is a desire to "show-off." Your strong Saturn influence will go far to protect you from this fault. You should also curb your masterfulness so that you may not seem dictatorial or over-bearing. These qualities do not sit well on anybody, least of all on a woman who is naturally of a warm and affectionate nature and attractive to the opposite sex.

Your planetary colors are yellow, orange, lead-gray and black; your flowers, the marigold and the peony; your stones, the diamond, the ruby, the lodestone, the topaz and all dark, unpolished gems. If these colors, flowers and jewels do not become you, you do not need to wear them; but if you do, you will have the satisfaction of knowing that you are dressing in harmony with your stars.

The Sun, which is the ruling planet of your sign and therefore the strongest influence in directing your choice of a profession, favors especially those in high positions either in commerce or statecraft. It is also particularly friendly to jewelers and all those who work in precious metals.

Saturn, on the other hand, lends its influence to more everyday labors. It favors mining, real estate, coal and wood business, dealing in lead products, plumbing—and, generally speaking, those occupations where success is won by the sweat of the brow and the strength of the hand.

You have, as you see, a wide field. The great thing is to choose the thing that seems most congenial to you!

If You Were Born Between August 3rd and August 13th—

Jupiter, the Greater Fortune, and the Sun, Giver of All Life, were dominant in the astrological heavens when you were born. And as if that wasn't enough for any one human being, your sign is Leo, symbolized by the Lion and known to astrologians as the Royal Sign.

Leo people make friends easily, and are social favorites because of their ability to charm by their personality. They are warm-hearted, very lovable, and ready to do battle against the world for the sake of their dear friends. They take as a personal injury any criticism of those dear to them.

Their desire for attention and compliments often amounts to a weakness and their great sensitiveness makes it difficult

for them to stand criticism.   Some of their greatest pleasure
comes through giving happiness to others.   They have very
youthful magnetism and they never grow old in spirit; as
they advance in life, they attract very young people as
friends, and who will help to keep them young and active.

You are in many ways among the most fortunate of Leo's
children. You not only possess the generous high-mindedness
typical of the sign and despise that which is petty or underhanded, but, thanks to Jupiter, you are also kind, generous,
sympathetic, humane.

Your planetary colors are sea-green, blue, purple, yellow,
violet and mixtures of red and indigo; your flowers, the
peony and the marigold; your stones, the amethyst, the emerald, the diamond, the ruby and the sapphire.   If these
colors, flowers and stones do not become you, you do not
need to wear them; but if you do, you will have the satisfaction of knowing that you are dressing in harmony with
your stars.

You are the center of your domestic circle.   You expect
the family to revolve around you; and it does.   However
modest your home, you convert it into a court—and rule it
as if by divine right!   You should succeed in almost anything you undertake, not only by your own merits—which
are great—but by inheritance or by marriage, or by fortunate
speculations.

If you are a man, your executive ability and your tireless
application to work fits you for the management of great
enterprises.   You are the ideal combination of managerial
ability and salesmanship.   In fact, many sales managers are
found in this sign.   Your forcefulness and your natural desire to dominate fit you for positions of high authority.
Presidents and managers of large corporations—captains of
industry—are very often Leo men.

The Sun, which is the ruling planet of your sign and the

most influential factor in directing your choice of a profession, favors especially those in high positions either in commerce or statecraft. It is also particularly friendly to jewelers and all those working with precious metals.

Jupiter, on the other hand, is an element for success, no matter what line of endeavor you choose. It, too, favors lawyers, judges, clergymen, physicians, bankers—important people generally; as well as clothiers, provision dealers, and all people engaged in the manufacture and sale of good things to eat and wear.

You are, you see, equipped to do well in many lines. Your executive ability plus your natural masterfulness makes success almost inevitable. But you must not forget that you may have some of the faults of your virtues. He who does a thing well usually likes to have others see how well he does it. The temptation to show-off one's really high abilities is at times too heavy to resist.

Resist this temptation, and also the temptation to dominate, and you should gain the high place in the world for which the stars have destined you!

If You Were Born Between August 14th and August 23rd—

When I tell you that you were born in the astrological sign, Leo, symbolized by the Lion; that the dominant influence in that sign is the Sun, Giver of All Life; and that the dominant planet in the heavens when you were born was Mars, the God of War, you will realise the responsibility which is on you to live up to your stars.

The sons and daughters of Leo are warm-hearted, overgenerous and sympathetic. They are inclined to be rather boastful, not only concerning their achievements, but also those of their family, their friends and their belongings. The fact that anything belongs to them makes it, in their eyes, tne best in the world. They are very unhappy if they cannot be first in a game, a contest, or in the esteem of their fellows. Unless this trait is tempered by good judgment, it often proves to be a stumbling block, as their associates resent their air of superiority and tendency to "show-off."

You, with your Mars influence, should especially realise that if you have done anything which is worthy of praise or merit, others will recognise it. It is not necessary for you to "blow your own horn."

A weakness of many people born under your stars is their desire to dominate others. You should realise that others desire freedom as well as yourself. You will be happiest when you feel responsibility, or are in a position of authority. A free expression of your nature will be absolutely necessary in order for you to be at your best, either physically or mentally.

You, as a child of Leo, are subject to all these influences and also to the vibrations of Mars, the planet which was dominant in the heavens at the particular time when you were born. But just because Mars is active in your horoscope, you are not necessarily warlike and quarrelsome. Mars gives his children energy, enthusiasm, initiative and power, as well as a tendency toward aggressiveness and strife.

Your planetary colors are blood-red, orange, scarlet, yellow-brown and yellow; your flowers, the marigold and the peony; your stones, the moon crystal, the chrysolite, the diamond and the ruby. If these colors, flowers and jewels do not become you, you do not need to wear them; but if you do, you will have the satisfaction of knowing that you are dressing in harmony with your stars.

You are careful in dress, but are not slave to the fashion of the moment; you adorn yourself because it is an expression of your pleasure in beautiful externals. You are very eager for the approval and compliments of others, and nothing makes you feel so satisfied as being appropriately dressed. Your desire for praise often causes others to take advantage of you by catering to this weakness. You should guard against the subtle influence of flattery and the assumption of an attitude which will make you seemingly over-confident of your own powers. You should try to be more detached in your feelings.

Like most Leo people, you should have a splendid constitution, but don't fail to take care of it. Look out especially for the heart and back. Add common-sense living to your natural vitality, and you won't go far wrong physically.

Many men born under Leo tend to excel as officers of large corporations, directors, superintendents, sales managers, captains and lieutenants of industry. You, with your Mars influences, should rise well above the ranks. And you will— if you go about it quietly, modestly, and with the least possible ostentation.

The Sun, which is the ruling planet of your sign and the most influential factor in determining your choice of a profession, favors especially those in high positions either in commerce or statecraft. It is also particularly favorable to jewelers and all those who work with precious metals.

Mars watches over soldiers, surgeons, chemists, dentists, barbers, workers in iron and steel and all those who use sharp instruments. And, of course, it favors the army, the navy and all warlike pursuits. So you see you have a wide field of interesting and important activities from which to choose your life work.

Whatever you do, remember that you belong to the Royal Sign—and that you must live up to it royally!

VIRGO

THE SIXTH SIGN

"Of science and logic he chatters,
As fine and as fast as he can;
Though I am no judge of such matters,
I'm sure he's a talented man."
                              —Praed.

VIRGO

AUGUST 24TH THROUGH SEPTEMBER 23RD

VIRGO the Virgin is the second sign of the Zodiac ruled by the planet Mercury. The first sign was Gemini. But so different is Virgo from Gemini and so different is its effect on everything with which it comes in contact that the casual astrological observer would scarcely recognise the planet as the same Mercury.

In Gemini, Mercury was light, airy, volatile and inclined to be undependable. Its nature was accurately described by the adjective now in common use, "mercurial." In Virgo, Mercury has come down to earth, as it should, since Virgo is an earth sign; and it has its feet planted firmly on the ground.

As a result, the native of Virgo is essentially a logical, systematic, sensible person. He is intellectual rather than emotional, practical rather than sentimental. He analyses himself and all those with whom he comes in contact. And he spares none.

The Virgin, which is the traditional symbol of Virgo, denotes the clarity of vision and the purity of the mental processes of the natives of this sign. The Virgo type sees the world eye-to-eye, as a child sees it before his vision has been clouded by emotional storms. With wide-eyed, unashamed curiosity, the Virgo native looks out on the world—and does not always find it good.

Those of us who have survived the innocence of childhood and the groping curiosity of adolescence realize that this old world of ours must not always be viewed without the aid of rose-tinted glasses; but the native of Virgo, for all his intellectual development, has not learned this lesson. Undismayed by the complexity of materials with which he has to work, he proceeds to separate and classify and arrange mankind according to his own logical and systematic ideas of what the world should be. He is not unfair in his appraisal. He recognizes values; and in his clear-minded way, he gives them just due—but no more. He seldom praises. He never over-praises.

If the Virgo mind were content to present the result of its analysis without comment, its possessor would be considered much more of "a good fellow" than is often the case. But Virgo people must criticize as well as analyze. Virgo's motives are the best. It wishes to be helpful, constructive. But its methods, unsoftened by emotion, sometimes have quite the opposite effect on those whose minds are less logical and less analytical. Virgo's criticism is usually true, but it usually hurts—and criticism that hurts seldom attains its end.

The possessor of such a high type of mentality assumes grave responsibilities for its use. If he applies it, as the undeveloped Virgo type is tempted to do, in a captious, cantankerous, aggravating way, he robs himself of the influence which he should have and he rouses in others impatience, irritability, ill-humor and defiance.

I put these dangers which beset the natives of Virgo first, because it is essential that they should recognize their existence and use their really great gifts in modifying or avoiding them. If they do, they blossom forth as the brightest flowers in the garden of the intellect. They make our most distinguished analytical writers, our most discriminating critics; in more everyday fields, they become our ablest organizers, our finest executives, managers and directors of vast enterprises.

There is no task too difficult for the Virgo native to attempt. There is no detail too small or too unimportant for him to study and to master. And this industry and devotion is not always spent on tasks, the performance of which will result in personal glory and profit. The natives of Virgo sometimes create the appearance of selfishness but it is chiefly an appearance.

They toil unremittingly in the service of others. They care much less about the rewards of work than they do about work itself. They are all too often slaves to duty and victims of detail. They do the work for which others get the credit. The Virgo native has also many desirable personal qualities which should contribute to his popularity. He is a just person. He deceives neither others nor himself. He is slow to anger. He is conscientious in everything he undertakes: if a woman, a good housekeeper; if a man, a good provider.

The problem of the Virgo native is to supplement these solid virtues with some of the lighter and more purely ornamental traits which contribute so much to social success. He cannot help observing defects which might escape a less critical person, but he can keep from voicing his criticism of these defects too publicly. It will do him no harm to cultivate the sympathetic, tolerant side of his nature, to remember to say an occasional word in appreciation and praise. It will be a good thing for him, too, if he keeps some of the details of his analysis—even his self-analysis to himself—and refrains from imposing on others the various systems which it is his pleasure to devise.

There are many successful marriages in which natives of Virgo have a part. They may be lacking in some of the emotional fire which lends glamor to courtship, but in the everyday life of the home their solid qualities often come into their own. Whenever possible, Virgo people should marry young before their critical tendencies have developed into crustiness and before their capacity for systematizing and organizing their lives has made them loathe to disturb their existence by sharing it with another. In the marriage relation, they must be especially careful to avoid imposing their ideas on the persons they love. More than most people, they must learn the principle of give and take. They get along especially with the natives of Taurus or Capricorn—but here, as always, it is impossible, without more knowledge of the individual horoscopes involved to lay down an infallible rule for marital success.

Virgo people are essentially healthy. They derive their strength from the earth; they have few temptations to excess, and it is well that this is so, for high living and deep drink-ing are especially disastrous for them. The chief danger to the health of the Virgo-born is over-work. Virgo people never spare themselves; in fact, their pride in their ability to perform more difficult tasks than the average human being is often their undoing. Virgo people are superlatively equipped to do the work of the world. They should keep themselves in condition to do it!

If You Were Born Between August 24th and September 2nd—

You are a child of Virgo. The astrological symbol of your sign is the Virgin; its dominant planet is Mercury, Messenger of the Gods. You are logical; you observe details that might escape the ordinary eye. You are critical of yourself and others. You have pride in your own abilities. You set a high standard for yourself. You are not conceited.

You have an inventive turn of mind. You lay out systems and solve problems by ingenious devices. You analyse every-thing, including yourself. You should remember that others are not so interested in what you think about yourself as you are.

Your planetary colors are green, yellow, gold, orange, blue and black; your flowers, the azalea, the lavender and the bachelor's button; your stones, the chrysolite, the jasper, the emerald, the topaz and the agate. If these colors, flowers and jewels do not become you, you do not need to wear them; but if you do, you will have the satisfaction of knowing that you are dressing in harmony with your stars.

If you are a woman, you are chaste and devoted, but inclined to be undemonstrative, even cold. You are more intellectual than emotional. You do not yearn for children, although you make the most conscientious of mothers.

If a man, develop expertness in theoretical or practical mechanics; and you will have success in pursuits where your analytical powers come into play. You have a gift for building, manufacturing, farming and mining. You do well in real estate. Virgo people make good accountants; some win success as teachers and writers.

Mercury, which is the ruling planet of your sign and the most influential factor in your choice of a profession, is especially favorable to all those engaged in the production of literature: not only writers but editors, publishers, printers and booksellers. It also governs interpreters, registrars, clerks and letter carriers.

The Sun, on the other hand, which was also dominant in the heavens when you were born shines with special favor on all those who occupy high positions either in commerce or statecraft; and is particularly friendly to jewelers and others who work with precious metals. So you see you have a wide field of interesting and important occupations from which to choose your life work.

You have a tendency to disorders of the liver, spleen and

pancreas. Be on guard also against gall stones, peritonitis, and typhoid fever. Avoid alcohol. There is no reason why you should have any of the troubles common to natives of your sign, if you select a plain diet and take good care of yourself otherwise.

If you wish the distinction which is within the reach of the highly developed Virgo person, you should try above all things to become a good mixer. Know your fellowmen and let them know you.

The Sun has an expansive effect on most people, but it gives the Virgo native born strongly under its influence a tendency to secretiveness. You should guard against it. The Sun, however, confers a long life and often an interesting one.

You should bear in mind these characteristics of your sign. Hold fast to their virtues, and soften their asperities. Do not be afraid to let yourself go!

If You Were Born Between September 3rd and September 12th—

Venus was the dominant influence in the astrological heavens at the moment of your birth. Mercury is the dominant planet of the sign Virgo in which you were born, but Venus rules that part of the sign in which your birthday falls.

This sign causes people who are born strongly under its influence to have a very practical side and to have aims which are usually impelled by some so-called material advantage. Unlike Gemini, they will have little interest in writing a book for its own sake, but would be influenced rather by the money or fame it would bring. The outlook of the Virgo type is thus apt to be rather narrow or one-sided and their reason hampered by the perpetual intrusion of the pragmatical standpoint. They should strive to broaden their conceptions and to overcome their natural tendency to be too self-satisfied; otherwise their great desire to teach purity and to raise the public morality and health will fail to materialize. But you, with your Venus influence, should be able to protect yourself against these dangers.

Your sign tends to make you over-fastidious in the selection of your friends and cold or indifferent to those you do not love or admire. You sometimes unconsciously throw out an atmosphere that repels others. By allowing Venus to help you soften your feelings a trifle, you will add to your own magnetism and to the joy you get out of life, as well as increasing your influence and giving more happiness to your friends. You would do well to practice giving freer expression to your more tender emotions.

Because of your great sense of the appropriate and the fitness of things, even more than because of your moral standards, you are in little danger of being indiscreet or unconventional. All of your senses are highly developed, and you see, hear, feel and smell things more acutely than the average mortal. For this reason you magnify the importance of trifles, are impatient with what appears to you to be stupidity, and are not only terribly exacting in dealing with yourself, but with others.

You must guard against expecting too much of your friends and should not attempt to make them over. Instead of seeing their faults and short-comings, you should try to magnify their virtues, realising that we all have our place in the scheme of the Universe. Although criticism may be an incentive to some, the average mortal accomplishes more when encouraged and given just praise. The softening influence of Venus should help you to cultivate a more sympathetic, tolerant, forgiving spirit and not allow your love of detail to master you or obscure your larger vision.

You are constructive, have splendid discrimination, perception and good judgment, but your tendency to lack decision may interfere with strict attention to the matter in hand. Many people born under your sign with really wonderful abilities fail to make good use of them because they have no fixed purpose. Therefore, you should try to cultivate stability of character and never make changes on impulse or because you are bored with existing conditions.

The Virgo-born should also cultivate concentration of mind; otherwise they may develop into dilettantes, "knowing everything and understanding nothing." Although they learn quickly, they often find it difficult to retain knowledge. Their sensitiveness to the influence of others makes it necessary that they decide on important subjects when quite alone. The first hours of the morning before they converse with anyone would be the best time.

The sons and daughters of Virgo are natural students of the laws of health and hygiene. They have a tendency to give too much thought to their physical condition and to study their symptoms so minutely as to be in danger of becoming hypochondriacs. They must learn not to depend too much on drugs, but realise that exercise in the fresh air, plenty of sleep and a contented mind will give them the greatest relief.

Your general health, however, should be good. Virgo people sometimes suffer from disorders of the liver, spleen and pancreas; also from gall stones and peritonitis; but if you avoid intoxicating liquor and stick to a plain diet, you should enjoy a long life.

Mercury, which is the ruling planet of your sign and the most influential factor in directing your choice of a profession, is especially favorable to all those engaged in the production of literature, not only writers, but editors, publishers, printers and booksellers. It also governs interpreters, registrars, clerks and letter carriers.

Venus, on the other hand, favors musicians, painters, actors, artists of all sorts. It is friendly to makers of toilet accessories, manufacturers of women's clothing and dealers in all kinds of articles of personal adornment; and also governs florists, confectioners and fancy bakers.

Your planetary colors are white, light blue, yellow, orange, slate-color and green; your flowers, the azalea and the bachelor's button and lavender; your stones, the green jasper, the beryl, the lapis-lazuli, the carnelian, the agate and the marcasite. If these colors, flowers and jewels do not become you, you do not need to wear them; but if you do, you will have the satisfaction of knowing that you are dressing in harmony with your stars.

If you are a woman, you should learn to be more natural in your attitude toward the man you love. Don't be over-critical. See their good side as well as their bad, and confine your conversation so far as possible to the former. Show the man you love that you have an emotional side as well as a practical one!

If You Were Born Between September 13th and September 23rd—

You were born in the intellectual sign Virgo, symbolized by the Virgin: and Mercury the planet which rules the intellect was dominant in the astrological heavens when you were born.

Your natural tendency is toward literature or some form of artistic expression bringing you into public notice. Your aspects are favorable for acquiring property, but your greatest reward may come through popular acclaim. You are well fitted for scientific study, especially in medicine and hygiene and the mechanical arts. Your versatility might find a congenial outlet in secretarial work, in teaching, in manufacturing, or in lines having to do with building and real estate. In anything you undertake, you have a keen eye for detail. You love to study a problem and to solve it by some device or system of your own. You are great on devices and systems. Don't follow this tendency too far; it will complicate your own life and burden other people's.

Mercury, the ruling planet of your sign and the chief factor in determining your choice of a profession, is especially friendly to all those engaged in the production of literature: not only writers, but editors, publishers, printers and booksellers. It also favors interpreters, registrars, clerks and letter carriers.

You are naturally orderly, but you are inclined to let little things overshadow the more important things of life. You should take small disappointments lightly; otherwise you will not be able to surmount greater trials or difficulties. It is very easy for you to become depleted nervously by worrying or fretting over petty annoyances; from a larger standpoint, however, you have a very hopeful and buoyant side, which should be developed.

You should have frequent rest periods, as you use up so much nervous force with your great mental activity. It is also essential that you should live in an atmosphere of calm and harmony and not be surrounded by excitable, exacting or nervous persons. You are not a spontaneous "mixer," and because of your indifference to others, you should be given an opportunity to cultivate your latent talents, in order that you may be less dependent on friends.

Your planetary colors are green, yellow-green, blue and black; your flowers, the bachelor's button, the lavender and the azalea; your stones, the marcasite, the agate, the jasper, the emerald and the topaz. If these colors, flowers and jewels do not become you, you do not need to wear them; but if you do, you will have the satisfaction of knowing that you are dressing in harmony with your stars.

Virgo governs the intestinal canal, the solar plexus and sympathetically the lungs and nervous system. Although this sign gives great endurance, provided the native heeds the laws of hygiene, it is most necessary that those born under its influence should give attention to the diet and should avoid neglecting any indications of intestinal poisoning, particularly during the month of September. Poor assimilation and appendicitis are also dangers of this sign. Too many sweets or rich and greasy food should be avoided, and the liver and intestines kept very active at all times, because they are in danger of suffering from all acute or chronic diseases of the liver.

You have the mentality and force to train yourself to present a more "social" side to the world than you usually show. You should do this, as it will increase your popularity with both sexes. Your tendency is to believe that you can hold a man's affection by good works alone. It can't be done. You must show your affection, even if it is a conscious effort for you to do so. Concentrate on the good points of the man you love—and tell him about them. Overlook the bad points—or if you can't do that, keep them to yourself!

LIBRA

THE SEVENTH SIGN

*"Poetic Justice, with her lifted scale,
Where in nice balance truth with gold
she weighs."*

—POPE.

LIBRA

SEPTEMBER 24TH THROUGH OCTOBER 23RD

LIBRA is the sign of Beauty; and, appropriately, it is ruled by Venus, the Goddess of Beauty.

But just as the Mercury that rules over Virgo is a different Mercury from the one that rules over Gemini, the Venus that rules over Libra is a very different Venus from the one that rules over Taurus. In Taurus, Venus is the Goddess of physical love, of the warm, vibrant affection which finds its ultimate expression in human passion. In Libra, Venus is the divine patroness of the arts, the symbol and the expression of esthetic beauty. And the children of Libra are consequently as different from the children of Taurus as the air is different from the earth; as the Scales from the Bull. The symbolism which accompanies the twelve signs of the Zodiac —the Ram for Aries, the Bull for Taurus, the Twins for Gemini, the Crab for Cancer, the Lion for Leo, the Virgin for Virgo and the Scales for Libra—is never more authentic or significant than it is in describing this sign of balance, therefore of symmetry, therefore of beauty. It is only when the world gets out of balance that it is ugly. When the scales tip neither this way nor that, justice prevails; and honour, and true beauty of living.

Mentally, therefore, the children of Libra are the judges, the arbiters, the guardians of fair play. They scorn caddish deceit, not because it is wrong, but because it is ugly. They refuse to stoop to grossness and debauchery, not because the sins of the flesh are outside any formal moral code, but because they disturb the eternal balance and symmetry of life.

Protected as they are by this cult of beauty-worship, the natives of Libra turn naturally and enthusiastically to the esthetic pleasures of life. The true son of Libra gets almost as much pleasure from a beautiful tree as he does from a beautiful woman. The true daughter of Libra worships not so much the man she loves as the picture of the man which she has painted on the canvas of her soul. These people thrill to sights which pass unnoticed in the surging life dominated for the most part by the courageously battling sons of Mars and the robustly prosperous sons of Jupiter. Their pleasures are the pleasures that are least understood by the crowd, and by this token, the children of Libra are the least understood of all the members of the Zodiacal family.

This baffling, fugitive Libra nature is not without its attractiveness in the realm of love. It possesses much of that idealism which constitutes the charm of the Aries lover without the disturbing aggressiveness imparted to the natives of that sign by its ruling planet Mars. It possesses the mental illusiveness, the divine lightness of touch, which renders the Gemini lover so annoying yet so intriguing. But over and above these borrowed attributes, it possesses its own incomparable sense of beauty which raises the humblest expressions of affection to the highest plane.

Libra does all these things; and yet, Libra lovers too often fail to satisfy and hold the object of their affections. In fact, it seems as though there were more Taurians in this world than Librans; at least more human beings who seek and appreciate the warm, friendly Taurian type of affection. The Libra lover treats his beloved as if she were a beautiful vase—and there are few women in this world content to be a vase, even a beautiful one. As for masculine vases, the type is well-nigh extinct!

Once the true mate is found, however, the possibilities for happiness in marriage with the Libra-born are inexhaustible.

To attain Harmony and to preserve it, the true Libra husband or wife will sacrifice everything. Peace, happiness, contempt—these are the stuffs of which the Librans' life are made; and these, as every married person knows, are the foundations on which a successful marriage must be built. The Libra woman is especially successful in this rôle of votary before the altar of domestic peace.

Libra people are not usually robust in appearance but invariably possess an extremely sound constitution. Being inclined to moods, they often worry about their health when there is no real cause to do so. The weak points that do need watching, however, are the kidneys and the lumbar regions, so it is well for them to avoid too violent exercise, especially if it involves a strain on the back.

Venus governs not only the social and love-interest side of the life of the Libra-born—with which her name is usually associated—but also confers success in more material matters. They may well be in a position to acquire property either in houses or land. They are clever in business matters; and when they back their cleverness with decision and force they are able to win a fair share of both fortune and fame. This necessity for using decision and force is an important factor toward achieving success in whatever line of work they eventually undertake, as they are always inclined to be controlled by the mood of the moment. It may be a mood of extreme mental elation or one of black depression. It is a natural inclination, though, for them to have both head and feet in the same place at the one time—in the air or on the ground—instead of letting their feet remain touching the firmness of the earth while their head, in air, is surrounded by the visions of esthetic and idealistic beauty which they so ardently worship. If only they learn the art of making up their mind toward a definite end, they can accomplish wonders. The most important thing for them to consider is that the profession which they choose should be congenial, as they must have harmonious surroundings to bring out the best that is in them in every way.

The watch-word of the sign Libra is Harmony!

If You Were Born Between September 24th and October 3rd—

You were born under that sign of the Zodiac symbolized by the Scales. Therein lies your strength and your weakness.

Just as it takes only a trifle to tip the scales one way or the other, so it is with those born under this sign. With their natures well under control, they are in perfect equilibrium and neither enjoy nor suffer to as intense a degree as the average mortal, but with their acute sensitiveness, a slight opposition or a little commendation depresses or elates their finely organized natures. The influence of the unstable Moon, which was dominant in the heavens when you were born, does not lessen those tendencies.

Libra people require the comforts of a home, but dislike to assume the responsibility of the married state; and not being unduly jealous themselves, cannot accustom themselves to being limited in their freedom. The pure Libra type is very esthetic, and holds a worshipful feeling toward those they love, which is not always wholly satisfying to the other person. The average individual prefers a more personal demonstration and does not enjoy feeling that he is placed upon a pedestal. This may have no serious effect on older or married people, but it can become a menace to young people, especially to young girls, by causing them to have early disappointments in love.

In matters outside of the affections, people born under your stars are enthusiastic and hopeful, so that disappointment or disaster cannot dishearten them. They are inherently honest and generous, more than ready to hold up their end; but expect the same treatment from others.

Venus, the ruling planet of your sign and the most influential factor in determining your choice of a profession, governs musicians, poets, painters, actors, artists of all kinds; also makers of women's apparel, manufacturers of toilet accessories and dealers in articles of personal adornment. It is friendly to florists, perfumers, bakers and confectioners.

The Moon, on the other hand, governs the public. It is friendly to salesmen and others dealing with large numbers of people. It helps all those who "go down to the sea in ships" either as sailing men or shipping merchants. It would favor your activities as an importer or exporter, as a dealer in liquids of any kind, or as a manager of transportation especially on water.

You should also do well in banking, diplomacy, engineering, law, architecture; in fact, in almost any artistic or professional career to which your special gifts may incline you. Venus governs not only that side of your life with which her name is usually associated, but also confers success in more material matters. You may well be in a position to acquire property either in houses or land.

You are by nature of a very sound constitution. Your powers of endurance and recuperation are great. Should ill health come upon you, guard against diseases of the kidneys and the lumbar region. Avoid violent exercise and straining the back.

Your planetary colors are white, pale yellow, pale green, light blue, and indigo; your flowers, the foxglove, the violet, the daisy and the lily of the valley; your stones, the moonstone, the sapphire, the opal, the crystal, the beryl, the green jasper and the coral.

In love, if you are a daughter of Libra, you have great power. You are able to adjust yourself readily to the demands of the man you love, especially if you have a motive. This ability gives you a great influence over him—and the kind of influence he should like!

If You Were Born Between October 4th and October 13th—

You are a native of Libra. You love beauty, harmony, symmetry, justice. You exemplify in your nature the Scales, which are the symbol of this sign.

Venus, Goddess of Love, is the dominant planet of all Libra people. Her influence accentuates many of the finer traits of the sign. Many musicians, painters, poets and actors have Venus prominent in their horoscopes.

You are exceedingly fond of your home and are by nature steadfast in your affections. But your domestic life may not always be serene. Saturn, the Celestial Schoolmaster, was very influential in the astrological heavens when you were born, and he may lead you through trials and tribulations to happiness. That is Saturn's way.

People born under Libra although naturally amiable, have a tendency to moods. They are up or down. They are too elated by temporary success, too depressed by temporary failure. Saturn is on the side of the second of these moods. So watch out for a tendency to easy discouragement and gloom. Don't be melancholy. And don't let your natural sensitiveness develop into super-sensitiveness. It will simply mean needless suffering and mental anguish, without gain.

In love you are an idealist. You have the finest sensibilities. You recoil from the crude; you tend naturally toward the exquisite. If you are not actively engaged in the arts yourself, you will enrich your life by an appreciation of them, and you will find your greatest happiness in association with artistic people.

Your planetary colors are green, dark-brown, lead-gray,

indigo, lemon-yellow, pale blue and white; your flowers, the foxglove, the violet, the daisy and the lily of the valley; your stones, the lodestone, the agate, the marcasite, the opal, the crystal, the carnelian and all unpolished blue or black gems.

Libra governs the loins, kidneys, organs of generation, spinal cord and the lumbar region; and, sympathetically, the head, stomach and knees. Watch out especially for ailments affecting these parts of the body. Avoid over-indulgence in sweets, and take plenty of exercise.

Venus, the ruling planet of your sign and the most influential factor in determining your choice of a profession puts her emphasis on the artistic side. She favors musicians, poets, painters, actors, artists of all kinds; also florists, perfumers, confectioners, manufacturers of toilet accessories, makers of women's apparel and dealers in articles of personal adornment.

Saturn, on the other hand, favors more work-a-day occupations: plumbing, undertaking, mining, dealing in coal or lead—in general, working by the sweat of the brow and the strength of the good right arm. So you see you have a wide field of interesting occupations from which to pick your life work. The thing to do is to find a congenial one and give to it the best that is in you.

Owing to Saturn's influence, your greatest success is likely to come late in life. When it does arrive, you will at least have the satisfaction of knowing that you deserve it and that it has been won by your own merits.

You see both sides of a question with extraordinary clearness. Your well-balanced mind fits you to decide fairly and wisely between them. What you must guard against is hesitation and delay in making your decision. Libra's traditional tendency to weigh things too long is accentuated in your case by Saturn's influence toward delay. Take yourself in hand.

Force yourself into action. Look out for your own interests. Stick up for your rights. Fight!

If You Were Born Between October 14th and October 23rd—

You were born under the astrological sign Libra, symbolized by the Scales. Venus, the Goddess of Love and
Beauty, is the dominant planet of that sign.

People born under Libra have a fine sense of harmony and
proportion. They are natural arbitrators. They make excellent judges, bankers, diplomats, architects and engineers.
They often succeed in artistic careers.

Venus, the Lesser Fortune, is the most influential factor in
your choice of a profession. Venus favors florists, perfumers,
confectioners, dealers in articles of personal adornment, manufacturers of women's apparel and makers of toilet accessories. It is also friendly to musicians, poets, painters, actors,
artists of all sorts.

Jupiter, the Greater Fortune, exerts an influence over you
second only to Venus's, and should bring you success in banking, politics, religion or the law. Jupiter's influence is a most
beneficent one and will help you in any line of work you
choose to adopt. With his assistance, you should overcome
that lack of decision and tendency to balance one side against
the other which often come between natives of Libra and
the greatest success.

Libra people are the best of company. This statement
applies with special force to those born in your part of the
sign, because Jupiter, which was influential in the astrological
heavens at the time of your birth, makes for popularity.

Your planetary colors are green, sea-green, blue, purple,
white, lemon-yellow, indigo, and violet; your flowers, the
foxglove, the daisy, the violet, and the lily of the valley;
your stones, the amethyst, the emerald, the sapphire, the pearl

the opal, the beryl, the green jasper and the lapis-lazuli. If these colors, flowers and jewels do not become you, you do not need to wear them; but if you do, you will have the satisfaction of knowing that you are dressing in harmony with your stars.

If you are a true son or daughter of Libra, you have the happy faculty of being able to see both sides of a subject and the ability to arrive at a just and merciful solution. You delight in making comparisons, contrasting shadow with sunshine, in order to discover the most excellent point of view. This quality may seem to indicate a lack of character, and in extreme instances may result in an unhappy inability to come to a decision. The favorable side of this trait is that it gives an endowment of broad view which is utterly opposed to bigotry and pettiness. The unfavorable side is that you just don't get things done. You must, therefore, force yourself to decision and action.

That last bit of advice is especially applicable to Libra women and their affairs of the heart. The daughters of Libra are experimenters in love. They have a great flair for it in all its finer and more delicate aspects, and they glory in trying all kinds. You, especially, with your Venus and Jupiter influences, are fitted to make a great success of love. Do not dilly-dally until it is too late. And when you do give yourself, don't be afraid to show your emotions.

The Libra-born are peculiarly sensitive to harmony and discord. They seem to have a subtle sense of the conditions about them. If these conditions are disturbed, they become sad or indifferent, even inconsiderate. They have a fondness for ceremonials; many high Church devotees are found in this sign and among the men are many Masons. Often they are distinctly psychic. When this force is controlled by common sense, it can be a valuable asset; if perverted, it becomes a source of unrest and misery. They are capable of developing along the highest lines of mentality, but must guard against feeling satisfied with superficial knowledge. They prefer inherently to accept the conclusions of established science rather than giving deep thought to or doing research work of their own. For this reason, when it comes to close application, you, as a child of Libra, may lose your enthusiasm and turn your attention to something new.

Your intuitions are very strong, but you are inclined to weigh things so carefully, feeling that there are always two sides to every question, that you frequently disregard your intuition for reason, much to your detriment in the long run. You must try to realise that usually your first impressions are more reliable than your carefully thought-out decisions.

Hesitation and indecision are your most serious limitations —but with Jupiter on your side you should fear nothing!

SCORPIO

THE EIGHTH SIGN

"Passion is power."
—Moody.

SCORPIO

"There was a little girl
And she had a little curl
That hung right down on her forehead.
When she was good,
She was very, very good,
And when she was bad, she was horrid."

I ALWAYS quote that nursery jingle to Scorpio people—
that is, people born between October 24th and November
22nd—because it seems to apply especially to them. Scorpio
is not only the strongest sign of the Zodiac, and the sexiest,
and the subtlest, but it also has the longest range. Every
sign has a symbol, but Scorpio has two: the Eagle and the
Scorpion. And it is fair that it should. For there is as
much difference between the developed and the undeveloped
Scorpio person as there is between the soaring eagle and the
lowly scorpion.

Theodore Roosevelt is the classic example of the highly
developed Scorpio man who transmuted the boundless energy
of his sign into strenuous living and vigorous achievement.
Robert Louis Stevenson and George Eliot, each in a different
way, overcame great handicaps with the help of this powerful sign. On the other hand, I could point to many lesser
known Scorpio people who have used the remarkable powers
of their sign in a most unfair manner. Scorpio is a strange
combination of strength and subtlety. The undeveloped

type is downright devious. He is almost invariably a hard
loser—and when he fights, he seldom fights fair.

So if you were born between October 24th and November
22nd, make sure you are an eagle, not a scorpion. Make
sure that you are tolerant and fair in your dealings with
others, that you do not blind yourself to your own faults
by egotism and senseless anger.

Much of the strength and some of the weakness of the
Scorpio character comes from the influence of Mars, the
ruling planet of the sign. Mars is a hot, dry, choleric, violent
planet. Its influence is often energizing and too often disturbing. Even in its most constructive phases, Mars is not a
calming factor in the horoscope. If you were born under its
influence (and you certainly were if you were born in the
sign Scorpio), you should make every effort to convert its
warlike, aggressive force into energy, initiative, enthusiasm
and courage, rather than into quarrelsomeness and strife.

Mars' influence contributes to the highly, or, if you will,
deeply passionate nature of some of the people born under
Scorpio vibrations. In love matters, Mars is the male as distinguished from Venus the female. Very few Scorpio men
suffer from lack of "it." Especially if a man has Venus in
this highly sexed sign, he is in trouble most of the time with
some woman or other. And not always very nice women,
either!

Now I have said so many unpleasant things about Scorpio
that I think it is time I said some pleasant things. And, of
course, it is easy to do so. As the distinguished author of
"From Pioneer to Poet" so well expressed it, "The kingdom to
which the son of Scorpio is called is a kingdom of power, and
his highest achievement is the manifestation of that power
in the most gigantic of tasks—absolute self-mastery. The
destruction of egotism, the domination of desire, the abolition
of everything that can retard his mental, moral and physical

regeneration; the attainment of complete control over the will, the intellect, the passions, the emotions, the bodily activities and the psychic faculties—these are, or ought to be, his ambitions, and very often he makes, in spite of false starts, failures and shortcomings, very considerable progress on the way to realizing them."

If you are a typical Scorpio person, you are capable of passionate devotion either to people or causes, but you are also inclined to folly and excess in affairs of the heart. You must control your passions and avoid extremes in these as in all other matters. If you don't you will stand a small chance of making a success of your marriage. These warnings are given, not to discourage you, but to point out the pitfalls so that you may be sure to avoid them. Incidentally, your most congenial mates may be found among the natives of Pisces or Cancer.

You have tremendous powers; and you owe it to yourself and to the world to learn how to use them. Your chief danger is that you will not adjust yourself to your surroundings and learn to appreciate and appraise your associates. If you don't allow your moods to make a slave of you or your temper to get the better of you, you should make a success of anything you seriously undertake. You don't need to worry if things go temporarily against you. With your ability, you should be able to recoup any loss and to turn any defeat into victory. Don't forget that you were born under one of the most powerful signs in the Zodiac, and that you are under obligation to use its powers for the common good.

You have a strong sense of discrimination, keep your own counsel, and are inclined to live very much within yourself. This is all very well provided it does not cause you to be misunderstood and distrusted. You are inclined to be critical of others but bitterly resent criticism of yourself.

Like most of the natives of your sign, you are shrewd and

penetrating. You have tremendous force, great driving power, and an analytical mind. You have a natural magnetism which should be a great asset to you, once you have schooled yourself to understand and appreciate the people with whom you are associated. Don't be over-critical of those who are not so richly endowed as you are. Control your anger. Avoid enmity, especially the secret enmity of women. Do not stoop to unfair methods. You don't need them to achieve success. Be a good loser. With your abilities you can soon recover your losses.

Above all, you should not allow yourself to become a prey to Scorpio's besetting sin, selfishness. You must not be so wrapped up in yourself that you cannot be sympathetic with your family and friends. You must seek to understand the people and the circumstances around you.

Scorpio people are usually endowed with robust constitutions which protect them from illness, and with great powers of recuperation; but if ill health does threaten, it is well for them to watch especially any unfavorable symptoms affecting the groin, the bladder, or the organs of generation.

As for your vocation in life, people born strongly under the influence of Scorpio have such a dominant will and strong personality that they are natural executives. Captains of industry, heads of large enterprises, sales managers, military and naval officers are often found under this sign; also many critics, journalists, musicians and chemists. Because of the complete coordination between their hands and their brains, and also because of their clear-headedness and detachment, they make capable surgeons, dentists, mechanical engineers, mining operators and machinists. They are "handy men around the house" and can do anything from driving a nail to tuning a piano.

Incidentally, more Presidents of the United States have been born under Scorpio than any other sign of the Zodiac!

If You Were Born Between October 24th and November 2nd—

The sign of the Zodiac under which you were born has two symbols, the Scorpion and the Eagle.

You are very strongly under the influence of this powerful and enigmatic sign, because Mars, God of War, which is the ruling planet of the whole sign was especially influential in the heavens at the time you were born. You are more Scorpio than most Scorpios. You may rise higher. You may fall lower.

Scorpio is a very strongly sexed sign; and, unlike Libra, stimulates more the physical sex than the esthetic. It may cause you to be a one-person individual so far as your affections are concerned, and inclined to be cold and indifferent to those who do not touch closely your personal life. Even though you give your personal devotion to one person, your ardor will soon cool, unless it is adequately reciprocated.

You may be so intense and absorbed in your love relations that you take the very attitude which drives away the object of your affections. Unless you are extremely discreet in your attitude toward the opposite sex, you will find yourself in most compromising situations, particularly with those beneath your station in life; in fact, inferiors will often fascinate you more than those in your own circle.

You are inclined to be critical of others, but bitterly resent criticism of yourself. If you are to succeed in a big way, you must cultivate a little more feeling for your fellow men. You must be tolerant of those who lack your ability to accomplish things. Learn to control your temper. And if you must fight, fight fairly.

With your abilities, backed by the tremendous force of your Mars influence, you can succeed at almost anything if you learn to control yourself. Scorpio people, however, are especially proficient as surgeons, critics, mechanicians, chemists and railroad officials.

Mars, the ruling planet of your sign and the most influential factor in determining your choice of a profession, favors soldiers, surgeons, dentists, barbers, and all those who use sharp instruments or work with iron, steel or fire. It extends its influence, however, far beyond the limits of those occupations, and makes for success in any line of work where courage, initiative, aggressiveness and executive ability count most heavily.

Your planetary colors are green-blue, blood-red, scarlet, crimson, all kinds of red; your flowers, the honeysuckle, the gentian, the broom and the red carnation: your stones, the topaz and the moon crystal. If these colors, flowers and jewels do not become you, you do not need to wear them; but if you do, you will have the satisfaction of knowing that you are dressing in harmony with your stars.

If you are a daughter of Scorpio, you are a one-man woman. You feel very strongly toward the person you love, but you appear cold and indifferent to others. Your ardor cools rapidly unless it is speedily reciprocated. You must guard against being attracted by your inferiors.

Most of the natives of your sign, especially those so strongly under Mars as you are, have pronounced traits which may be virtuous or vicious. In either state, however, they will be strong, for all things which concern them are persistent and consistent. There is no suggestion of enervation about them. They are never milk-and-water people!

If You Were Born Between November 3rd and November 13th—

You were born under the astrological sign Scorpio, symbolized by the Scorpion and the Eagle. Mars, the God of

War, is the ruling planet of this sign.   And the Sun, Giver
of All Life, was dominant in the heavens when you were
born.

People born under those planetary influences have such a
dominant will and strong personality that they are natural
executives, captains of industry, heads of large enterprises,
sales managers, military and naval officers.

Mars, the ruling planet of your sign and the most influential factor in determining your choice of a profession,
favors a good many of these activities.   It governs soldiers,
surgeons, chemists, dentists, barbers and all others who work
either with sharp instruments or iron, steel and fire.   It
also helps in any line of business where courage, initiative
and executive ability are the prime requisites.

The Sun, on the other hand, shines most brightly on people
in high positions either in commerce or statecraft.   It is especially friendly, also, to jewelers and all others who work with
precious metals.

Scorpio rules the groin, bladder and organs of generation,
and sympathetically the heart, throat and circulation.   Diseases affecting these organs, and those which come as a result
of drawing too heavily on the vital forces, may be contracted
if the laws of nature are abused.   In case of infection, the
sinus will frequently be affected.   Scorpio does, however,
give a robust constitution and great power of recuperation,
with every promise of splendid health, provided its natives
live normally.   If they live a too sedentary life they are likely
to suffer from poor circulation.

The undeveloped Scorpio-born are very skeptical and
materialistic; when they are once awakened, however, they
develop into true believers and even mystics.   Because of their
keenness and astuteness and their ability to take in everything without apparently making any effort to do so, they
often make excellent detectives, or writers of detective stories.

They are also "handy men" about the home, and can do anything from driving a nail to tuning a piano! Much of their magnetism is in their hands, and for this reason, they are also very successful as masseurs and nurses.

You, as a child of Mars and the Sun, should have a great deal of grit and determination to succeed. You should be able to lay aside all personal feeling and to execute the task in hand, regardless of danger or of interference. The reciprocal action existing between your mind and your nerves gives you firm touch and delicate dexterity, which should enable you to undertake and carry through successfully anything requiring nervous control.

Your planetary colors are gold, yellow, yellow-brown, all kinds of red, green-blue, and orange; your flowers, the gentian, the honeysuckle, the red carnation, and the broom; your stones, the chrysolite, the moon crystal, and the topaz. If these colors, flowers and jewels do not become you, you do not need to wear them; but if you do, you will have the satisfaction of knowing that you are dressing in harmony with your stars.

When engaged in serious matters, you are so firm and concentrated you unconsciously assume an air of superiority and command, which is not infrequently resented, but which is nevertheless convincing and inspires confidence in your associates. You need never worry about your ability to master others. You were born for that. Your only problem is to master yourself!

If You Were Born Between November 14th and November 22nd—

You are a Scorpio person. And Scorpio is one of the strongest signs in the Zodiac, and one of the most enigmatic. It is symbolized by the Scorpion and the Eagle—a combination which gives a fair idea of the possible scope of the sons of this sign.

All Scorpio people are strongly under the influence of the planet Mars; and Mars, even in its more constructive phases, is not a calming factor in your horoscope. You should make every effort to convert its warlike, aggressive force into energy, initiative, enthusiasm and courage, rather than into quarrelsomeness and strife.

Venus was also dominant in the astrological heavens at the time you were born, so you should be capable of passionate devotion either to people or causes. But don't be inclined to folly and excess in affairs of the heart. You must control your passions and avoid extremes in these as in all other matters. If you don't, you will stand small chance of making a success of your marriage.

These warnings are given not to discourage you, but to point out the pitfalls so that you may be sure to avoid them. As a true son of Scorpio, you are shrewd and penetrating. You have a tremendous force, great driving power, unusual discrimination and an analytical mind. You have a natural magnetism which should be a great asset to you, once you have schooled yourself to understand and appreciate the people with whom you are associated.

Don't be over-critical of those who are not so richly endowed as you are. Control your anger. Avoid enmity, especially the secret enmity of women. Do not stoop to unfair methods; you don't need them to achieve success. Be a good loser. With your ability you can recoup any loss.

Unless you have some special gift, such as music, you might do well to turn to the fields in which Scorpio people have always found success: railroading, chemistry, applied mechanics, surgery, and, of course, any military or naval activity.

Mars, the ruling planet of your sign and the most influential factor in determining your choice of a profession, governs many activities. It favors soldiers, surgeons, chemists, dentists, barbers and all others who work with sharp instruments or with iron, steel and fire.

Venus, on the other hand, favors florists, perfumers, confectioners, musicians, painters, poets, actors, artists of all sorts; also dealers in articles of personal adornment, makers of toilet accessories and manufacturers of women's apparel.

Your planetary colors are red, green-blue, light blue and white; your flowers, the gentian, the honeysuckle, the red carnation and the broom; your stones, the lapis-lazuli, the carnelian, the coral, the beryl, the sapphire, the topaz and the moon crystal. If these colors, flowers and jewels do not become you, you do not need to wear them; but if you do, you will have the satisfaction of knowing that you are dressing in harmony with your stars.

Scorpio rules the bladder, the groin and the generative organs. Protect yourself against ailments affecting these parts of your body. Avoid intoxicating liquors and dissipation of all sorts. But, in general, don't worry about your health. You have a strong constitution—an able body in which to house an able mind.

SAGITTARIUS

THE NINTH SIGN

*"Like an arrow shot
From a well-experienced archer hits the mark
His eye doth level at."*
—SHAKESPEARE.

SAGITTARIUS

NOVEMBER 23RD THROUGH DECEMBER 22ND

IF Jupiter is with you, nobody can be against you!

I say this over and over to my clients. And I say it now to all of you who may be born between November 23rd and December 22nd. For that is the period which is governed by Sagittarius, the sign of the Zodiac which is symbolized by the man with the arrow. And Sagittarius, in turn, is ruled by the beneficent planet, Jupiter.

Jupiter stands for success, wealth, position, glory. It is called in astrological language, "The Greater Fortune." Jupiter makes its sons and daughters noble, magnanimous, jovial, affable, temperate, wise. Against these qualities even the most adverse astrological aspects can make little progress. So, if you are a Sagittarian—that is, if you were born between November 23rd and December 22nd—you have in Jupiter an exceedingly powerful friend at the heavenly court. And besides all that, you are in a mighty good sign on its own account.

The typical Sagittarian is "the young man who sees visions and the old man who dreams dreams." But he is capable of seeing the outcome of a transaction before you may know that it is under way. The nature of his mind is typified by the ancient pictorial representation of Sagittarius as a centaur, with bow outstretched as if he was about to speed an arrow to its mark. Directness is the Sagittarian's line and he usually hews to it!

He makes friends quickly and is loyal to those to whom he becomes attached. The same qualities are present in his relations with members of the opposite sex. If a Sagittarius man finds a woman who really understands him, his nature will expand to its highest and best and he will make a devoted and appreciative husband. He cannot tolerate petty restrictions and unreasoning jealousy.

He is direct in speech and despises circumlocution in others. Nothing so angers him as duplicity. But his anger is short-lived, and he seldom bears malice. He is unselfish, direct and fearless. He should not be made unhappy through having his natural feelings suppressed or his exuberance checked. His recreational life should be favored, too. Sagittarius governs outdoor life and sports, especially sports which have to do with horses and dogs.

In love the Sagittarian-born is more idealistic than passionate. He is essentially very high-minded. He recoils from anything gross or sensual. He gives the purest kind of love and expects only the purest love in return. His ideals are so high in these matters that he is often accused of being lacking in sex. In fact, Sagittarius is sometimes called the "Bachelor Sign." But if it is true that there are more bachelor men and women born under this sign than any other, it is not due to any lack of physical attraction or appreciation. It is due chiefly to downright fastidiousness.

It is true that broken engagements abound among natives of this sign. This is the result of a conflict which goes on in the breasts of the Sagittarius-born between impulsiveness and caution. The Sagittarian frequently engages himself too soon, and lives to regret it. Some people, of course, would suffer in silence or wait for a favorable opportunity to slip away. But not so the Sagittarian. He comes right out and says that he was wrong, and he isn't always as tactful as he might be in the way he says it.

Another reason why the Sagittarian lover is not so successful in some instances as his really fine qualities deserve is that he does not give enough attention to the niceties of romance. Women like to be courted. Some even prefer insincere flattery to no flattery at all. It is too bad that there are these artificial barriers between the Sagittarius lover and the consummation of his love, because no one is in greater need than he of emotional development to bring out the best that is in him.

If a Sagittarian finds a member of the opposite sex who really understands the fine qualities which lie below his blunt and often brusque exterior, he makes an ideal husband. He resents jealousy and restriction; but his anger, though quick, is seldom long-lived; and he never cherishes a grudge. If he is sure that the woman of his choice is dealing openly and squarely with him, he will expand and develop. His flirtations, if they occur, are bound to be public ones and of slight importance.

The Sagittarian woman possesses most of these traits, both good and bad. If they follow their splendid intuition, they make excellent wives—provided always that they subdue their tendencies to bluntness in dealing with their husbands. They must be frank, because it is their nature, but they must be tactful, too.

In the world of affairs, if you are a true Sagittarian, you should go far because of your powers of intuition and insight. You are at your best in a sudden emergency which might overwhelm a person who depended on logical thinking alone. You should learn to put your trust in this power. Encourage this great gift that nature has handed you. In other words, play your hunches. Do not carry the thing to the point of rashness, but think twice before you accept the advice of others when it runs contrary to your own instincts. When the flash comes, trust it implicitly.

You are high-strung, proud, and naturally fastidious. You are sensitive to slights, real or imaginary, and are easily injured; but on the other hand you are not as careful as you should be of the feelings of others. You are inclined to be blunt, sometimes brusque and tactless. You should cultivate more diplomacy and learn to respect the feelings of those with whom you are thrown.

You will succeed best as a banker, broker, manager, organizer, political worker, or in some line where similar abilities are requisites of success. You should do well in athletics, especially in anything which has to do with horses or dogs. You have an excellent constitution, but you should look out for symptoms of sciatica and gout and ailments of the hips and thighs. Take plenty of exercise, and avoid rich or fried foods.

You are capable of great concentration, but lose interest when what you are doing is interrupted. You will succeed by combining your intuitive powers and your brilliant nature on something that will grasp and hold your entire interest. If you succeed in achieving this coordination and concentration, you will go far!

If You Were Born Between November 23rd and December 2nd—

You are a native of Sagittarius: frank, open-hearted, sincere. You love to talk and hate to listen. You speak the truth and expect truthfulness from others. Nothing angers you so quickly as duplicity. The symbol of your sign is a Centaur shooting an arrow straight to its mark. Directness is your line—and you hew to it.

In your avocations you are of a philosophic turn of mind. Your interests run to science, history, the humanities. In your vocation, if you have one, you should excel as an organizer or director of large enterprises, as a financier or statesman.

Jupiter, the ruling planet of your sign and the most influential factor in your choice of a profession, favors bankers, lawyers, judges, clergymen, statesmen, all those in positions of authority and power. It is also friendly to woolen merchants and provision dealers. But it makes for success in any line of work which you may adopt.

Mercury, on the other hand, which was also influential in the heavens when you were born, looks with special favor on those engaged in the production of literature: not only writers but editors, publishers, printers and booksellers. It is also friendly to accountants, clerks, registrars, letter carriers, interpreters and teachers.

Few people have a wider field from which to choose their life work. Your job is to select the one which is most congenial to you. And another thing: take plenty of vacations. Don't try to make a plodder of yourself. No true Sagittarian ever succeeded that way.

Go in for sports and games. You ought to be good at them, especially anything involving horses or dogs. Take plenty of exercise. Stay outdoors. Eat simply. Avoid gout, sciatica, ailments of the hips and thighs. But don't worry too much about your health. Your disposition may be nervous, but your constitution is sound.

Your planetary colors are blue, black, orange, slate-color, sea-green, violet and purple; your flower, the goldenrod; your stones, the turquoise, the diamond, the carbuncle, the amethyst, the emerald, the sapphire, the agate and the marcasite. If these colors, flower and jewels do not become you, you do not need to wear them; but if you do, you will have the satisfaction of knowing that you are dressing in harmony with your stars.

Some of the qualities of frankness which make you a fine friend are not so useful in affairs of the heart. You are not by nature romantic. You are more apt to choose your mate by logic than by feeling. Your extreme honesty makes you loath to enter into the little reticences which are necessary in most love affairs to keep the feelings from being hurt. But if you find a person who really understands and appreciates you, you make a devoted and loyal mate.

You are especially fortunate in being a child of Jupiter, the noblest of the planets, and called by astrologers "The Greater Fortune," because it presides over honor, glory, wealth and success, and imparts to those it favors the qualities of benevolence, generosity, sincerity and spirituality. Of course, Jupiter, like all the planets, is sometimes afflicted, and at such times we must be on the watch for losses from extravagance, wastefulness, and ostentation; but when Jupiter is beneficent, it increases our chances of good luck; it often brings honors, spiritual enlightenment, worldly influence and gratified ambition.

You are intuitive, almost clairvoyant. You are at your best in emergencies which would overwhelm a person who depended on logic alone. You have flashes and you follow them. You have hunches and you play them. And on the whole, you do well to do so. Your feelings about a person or a situation are often better than another fellow's thoughts.

You are a highly sensitive person, but not always considerate of the sensitiveness of others. Avoid brusqueness. Strive for tact. Don't be a man or woman of many enemies and some friends. Use your great gifts to tip the scales the other way!

If You Were Born Between December 3rd and December 12th—

You were born under the astrological sign Sagittarius, symbolized by the Centaur. Jupiter is the ruling planet of this sign. The Moon was also a dominant influence when you were born. It would be hard to imagine a more interesting and promising combination of celestial influences. So, if you are not the success the stars willed you to be, it must be your own fault!

Your planetary colors are white, pale yellow, pale green, sea-green, blue and purple; your flower, the goldenrod; your stones, the opal, the moonstone, the crystal, the emerald, the sapphire, the amethyst, the diamond and the topaz. If these colors, flower and jewels do not become you, you do not need to wear them; but if you do, you will have the satisfaction of knowing that you are dressing in harmony with your stars.

You are the breezy type of lover rather than the romantic. Your friends of the opposite sex are pals, comrades, chums. You demand many friendships outside the family circle. Personal freedom is your dominant passion. It may cause some difficulties if you are married to a person who is either very romantic or very jealous. You should strive to bring out the softer side of your nature. And, above all things, you should not be blunt or tactless in your conversations with the person you love.

Jupiter is the planet which confers honors, position, success, wealth. The Moon translates these qualities in terms of the public. You should win fortune, perhaps renown as a statesman, financier or Captain of Industry. You are eminently fitted by your natural endowment for organizing or directing large enterprises. Jupiter makes for success in any line of work you may adopt, but it is especially friendly to lawyers, bankers, judges, clergymen, statesmen and all others in positions of power and authority.

The Moon also favors a public career of some sort. A good many successful salesmen are born strongly under its influence. The Moon governs liquids, waterways, transportation, shipping, sailing, fishing, and all other activities having to do with water.

Whichever one of these many occupations you choose, do not try to make a plodder out of yourself. You are the kind that has flashes of inspiration. Call it insight, intuition, clairvoyance or simply "hunch"—you have it. And it will prove the greatest factor in your success. Don't yield to stray impulses, but when the real flash comes, trust it implicitly. Follow the light which the stars have given you.

Like most people born under Sagittarius, you are inclined to be nervous, high-strung, over-sensitive. Your feelings are easily injured—especially by slights, real or imaginary. This fact should make you more considerate of the feelings of others. Your impulsiveness sometimes reacts upon yourself. You drop the thing you are doing before it is finished. You should school yourself to patience and tenacity.

Being so well-balanced and normal, you should enjoy excellent health, unless you eat unwisely or expose yourself to contagious or infectious diseases. Even then, you throw off disease very readily and have splendid recuperative power. It is essential that you are not made unhappy through suppression of your feelings or having your natural enthusiasm and exuberance of feeling checked.

You should be a free soul!

If You Were Born Between December 13th and December 22nd—

You are a true son of Sagittarius. But in your case the influence of that inspirational sign and its ruling planet, the beneficent Jupiter, is modified and in some ways strengthened by the heavenly disciplinarian, Saturn. Therefore, you are more deeply serious than many of your fellow Sagittarians. You have a philosophical mind and a sober temperament. You have a taste for researches, in the field of philosophy and natural science.

Like most people born under Sagittarius, your real friendships are few but steadfast. You have the magnetism to draw people to you, but a tendency to brusqueness of manner and bluntness of speech drives a good many away. Your real nature, thanks to Sagittarius's frankness and openheartedness and Jupiter's genial humanity, is a most attractive one. You should try to show it to best advantage by concentrating on consideration for others. You are highly sensitive yourself. Remember that others are also.

In love and marriage you are inherently loyal. You despise licentiousness of any kind, and turn naturally to things that are pure and chaste. You must be appealed to on your mental and spiritual side before you can give your heart to anyone. Otherwise you soon become indifferent and feel that you are not getting enough in return for giving up your freedom.

Your planetary colors are green-blue, blue, black, dark brown, purple, violet, and mixtures of red and indigo; your flower, the goldenrod; your stones, the diamond, the topaz, the lodestone and all unpolished blue and black gems. If these colors, flower and jewels do not become you, you do not need to wear them; but if you do, you will have the satisfaction of knowing that you are dressing in harmony with your stars.

You are not so nervous and high-strung as many of the sons and daughters of your sign. You have less excuse than they for suffering through over-sensitiveness or for hurting and estranging others by impulsive and tactless actions. You are capable also of concentration. Make sure that you use your capability. Don't make yourself a slave to plodding routine—you are not that kind—but do learn to finish one thing before you begin another. You have brilliance. Learn application. Let your light shine in the right place.

Your natural inclination is toward literary or philosophical pursuits. There is every indication of success in these fields, especially literature. This does not mean, however, that you cannot excel in more practical lines: banking, managing, directing, organizing, financing, legislating.

Jupiter, the ruling planet of your sign and the most influential factor in determining your choice of a profession, favors bankers, lawyers, judges, clergymen, statesmen, all persons in positions of authority and power; but it extends its beneficent influence into any line of work which you may adopt. Saturn, on the other hand, governs more everyday activities such as plumbing, undertaking, mining, and dealing in coal or lead.

The athletic side of your nature should not be neglected. If you are not living part of your time in an atmosphere of wholesome outdoor sport and fun, you are not fulfilling your destiny. You may find pleasure in horses and dogs. You have a naturally strong constitution. If you take good care of your diet, look out for gout, sciatica and ailments which affect the hips and thighs, you should have a long and successful life.

You are a true Sagittarian. You have intuition. Don't turn your back on it. Inspired by Jupiter and disciplined by Saturn, your instinct is your best guide. Trust it!

CAPRICORN

THE TENTH SIGN

"That which ordinary men are fit for, I am qualified in; and the best of me is diligence."

—SHAKESPEARE.

CAPRICORN

DECEMBER 23RD THROUGH JANUARY 20TH

NOBODY likes to be the goat. Yet, approximately one twelfth of the human race is just that. At least, it is born under that sign of the Zodiac known as Capricorn the Goat. And the natives of this sign—that is, persons born between December 23rd and January 20th—partake of many of that excellent animal's characteristics.

However, the Capricorn-born do not always receive the credit they deserve—even from astrologers!—because their sign is one of the most difficult in the Zodiac to write about— not that it is so bad; far from it!—but it *sounds* bad. And there isn't any honest way of making it sound better.

Capricornians are often considered too practical or lacking in sentiment. They are very magnetic and fond of the opposite sex, but tend to be too physical in the expression of their love and to be very sudden and capricious in their likes and dislikes. Although indifference stimulates the average person, the Capricorn-born never fall in love until they are sure that their love is reciprocated.

They sometimes form attachments which sway the nature most powerfully, but they are capable of changing to icy indifference if their pride is hurt. They place too much importance on worldly advantages and are inclined to be very jealous and exacting with those they love. They should try and stimulate the more tender emotions and realise that the more unselfish they are toward others, the greater will be their own happiness and popularity.

Because of their natural industry, their willingness to plod, their accuracy, their inordinate ambition to rise above their environment and their ceaseless desire to get ahead, the Capricorn-born generally make a financial success of their lives. They often find that they meet with the most ready success as manufacturers, wholesale clothiers, builders, realtors, miners, agriculturists and foresters. There is quite another type born under this sign, usually possessing a more specialized education, which makes excellent educators, biologists, politicians, public speakers and historians. Gladstone and the late President Wilson are two pertinent examples of this type.

There is no sign that causes people to suffer so acutely from a feeling of being dependent upon others as does Capricorn; and for this reason, even at an early age, Capricorn people should be prepared for some constructive work, which will place them in a position to earn their own living, even if it does not seem necessary at the time. All through life, they are likely to err on the side of assuming too much responsibility regarding the destiny of others. They should bear in mind that it is best for all concerned to allow those with whom they are associated to work out their own salvation, as this is an age when everyone, consciously or unconsciously, is reaching out to be economically free.

Capricornians are born workers; they serve, but are not servile. They have a sense of direction and do not need to ask the way. Like the goat, they pick their footing for themselves and find their own path to the goal. They make the best of their circumstances and their capabilities. They plan well and make both ends meet. Although not one in a million may be a real miser, those born under this sign have the faults which lead to parsimony late in life, and those which give an inclination to drive a sharp bargain. Prudence and caution are salient characteristics of these people. They feel the way and test the ground thoroughly before trusting their full weight upon it. They are too practical to be caught in visionary undertakings. They have few, if any, "pipe dreams."

Those born strongly under the influence of this sign have an inherent tendency to despondency and melancholia, and their fear and dread of the future increases their inclination to lay up for a "rainy day." They should remember the old adages that "God helps those who help themselves," and to "trust in Providence, but keep your powder dry."

The path of those born under Capricorn is beset with obstacles and seemingly unsurmountable difficulties which their caution and industry convert into useful stepping stones. The men of this sign often seek distinction and supremacy in the political world. They seldom embark upon any enterprise which does not promise adequate return. They are capable of being successful leaders and can organize and carry on any stupendous undertaking incidental to their calling.

Both men and women have a great desire for knowledge, and through experience gain much wisdom. They look up to and revere those who are more learned than themselves, but often forget that machine-like accuracy has little personal value unless combined with wisdom.

The Capricorn people at times seem to stand still, but these periods of calm deliberation may be likened to the pause which the hare can afford in a race with the tortoise. They can afford to rest since in action they are rapid and direct. They are fond of travelling and in their journeyings frequently meet by chance with those who help them on their upward way. Their determined ambition to get ahead is so obvious that at times it becomes obnoxious and causes them to encounter enmity from those in high places, who may be jealous of their success, and also those in the lower social scale, who are envious.

Undeveloped Capricornians are self-assertive, selfish, sus-

picious, headstrong and subject to great extremes of mood
and peculiarities of temperament. Because they lack natural
buoyancy to help buck them up, they frequently resort to the
use of liquor or drugs for relief. There are more secret
drinkers born under the influence of Capricorn than any
other sign. The Taurus-born are sometimes heavy drinkers,
too; but they are so more because of a spirit of conviviality
and to be a "good fellow" than because they feel the need
of a drink as a mental or physical stimulant. Capricornians
should watch this tendency.

Lastly, the Capricorn-born should cultivate faith in themselves and the Universe and feel that their future depends
largely upon the use they make of the present. They should
not allow themselves to waste time and energy in crossing
bridges before they get to them. Their worst troubles never
happen!

*If You Were Born Between December 23rd and January
1st—*

You were born under the astrological sign Capricorn, sym-
bolized by the Goat. The ruling planet of this sign is Saturn.
The dominant planet at the moment you were born was
Jupiter.

The natives of Capricorn are usually true to the symbol of
their sign. Like the mountain goat, they are always climbing
toward the summit, overcoming every obstacle by persistence, endurance and ambition.

You as a native of this tenacious sign, attach the greatest
importance to marriage, but you must exercise finesse to
make a success of it. Strive to keep your affections on a
spiritual plane. Do not be capricious in your likes and dislikes. Make sure that secret evil does not threaten your fair
name.

In love, you may be too self-centered. There is also danger that you may be over-bearing or unsympathetic with children. You should watch these tendencies and see that they do not come between you and those you love.

Your planetary colors are ash-gray, green, black, brown, maroon, purple, violet and indigo; your flowers, the poppy, the flax and the holly; your stones, the onyx, the moss agate, the garnet, the lodestone, the emerald, the sapphire and the amethyst.

If you are a true child of Capricornus, you have industry, perseverance, and caution. In fact, you may have too much caution. For in spite of all the strength-giving qualities inherent in your sign and the beneficent influence of your own planet, Jupiter, your mind is often beset by unreasoning doubts. Don't let caution degenerate into foolish fear or a weakening sense of impending failure. Your greatest success will probably come late in life.

In religious matters you incline to strict sectarianism and to an austerity which amounts almost to self-immolation. Like most people born under Capricorn, you have strong domestic instincts. You love anniversaries and family gatherings of all sorts. You make an excellent host.

Industry backed by ambition can win success in almost any line where hard work is the chief essential to success. Capricorn men are especially proficient as manufacturers, builders, miners, foresters, and real estate dealers. Many statesmen are born under this sign.

Saturn, the ruling planet of your sign and the most influential factor in determining your choice of a profession, favors the more work-a-day activities such as plumbing, undertaking, mining, dealing in coal or lead.

Jupiter, on the other hand, governs judges, lawyers, bankers, clergymen, statesmen and all those in positions of power and authority. Jupiter is also friendly to woolen merchants and provision dealers. But the great thing about this beneficent planet is that it makes for success in any line of work you may adopt.

If you are a true son or daughter of Capricornus, you have great physical powers and an iron constitution. When illness threatens, look well to the digestive tract. Guard against rheumatic inflammations. Drink plenty of water. Avoid rich foods. Remember, your success will come from hard work. Keep yourself in condition to do it!

If You Were Born Between January 2nd and January 11th—

You were born under the ambitious, purposeful, industrious sign Capricorn. And everything that is true of your sign is apt to be doubly true of you. For Mars was dominant in the heavens when you were born and gives you added energy, initiative, enthusiasm and aggressiveness. With moderation added to your more warlike qualities, you should win high honor and wide fame.

As a true child of Capricorn, you are a born worker. Your energy is tireless, your ambition insatiable. You long for power. You value both knowledge and wealth for the power it gives you. You attract friends in high places. You get your share of the world's favors. You are surrounded by rivals, but you prevail over them.

Don't take life too seriously. And don't let your fear of some future catastrophe make you unwilling to enjoy the present to the full.

Your planetary colors are green, black, dark brown, blood-red, scarlet, green-blue, ash-gray and indigo; your flowers, the poppy, the holly and the flax; your stones, the moon crystal, the onyx, the garnet and the lodestone. If these colors, flowers and jewels do not become you, you do not need to wear them; but if you do, you will have the satisfaction of knowing that you are dressing in harmony with your stars.

If you are a true daughter of Capricorn, you have a strong love nature which will not be satisfied without a husband and a home. You have a deep family love and a high respect for the position of the home; but you must not be overbearing with those you love.

The climbing goat mounting towards the summit, overcoming all difficulties in the way, exemplifies some of the most striking characteristics of those born under the influence of Capricorn. They have pluck, persistence and tenacity. Whether they have reached the highest plane of their spiritual life or are still on the way, these qualities of forging ahead are always the same.

You should choose a calling in which these gifts are of prime importance. If you are a man, you will succeed in mining, farming, manufacturing, building, planning—in almost any occupation requiring patient, tireless application. You may excel in statecraft and military affairs.

Saturn, the ruling planet of your sign and the most influential factor in determining your choice of a profession, favors the everyday professions such as plumbing, mining, undertaking, dealing in coal or lead—anything where work is done by the sweat of the brow and the strength of the good right arm.

Mars, on the other hand, governs soldiers, surgeons, chemists, dentists, barbers and all those who work with sharp instruments or with iron, steel and fire. Mars is influential, also, in any other line where initiative, courage or executive ability are requisites of success.

As with Aries, Cancer and Libra, the other three cardinal signs, people born under the influence of Capricorn will find it necessary to give the strictest attention to the selection of their diet and to their elimination. They are peculiarly susceptible to inflammatory conditions, especially of a rheumatic character. They should not dwell upon their troubles, real or imaginary, because to do so would very easily bring on nervous dyspepsia or headache, and interfere with their health or even their success. They should seek the companionship of cheerful people. Saturn can do with a good deal of cheering-up!

If You Were Born Between January 12th and January 20th—

The Goat, symbol of the astrological sign in which you were born, is a much maligned animal. But, he has many excellent qualities: ambition, patience, tenacity, industry. He overcomes obstacles. And these qualities are prominent in most of the people of his sign, the forceful, purposeful Capricorn.

Saturn, the ruling planet of this sign, is known as the Celestial Schoolmaster. His influence is disciplinary and sobering, inclining toward melancholy. You must guard yourself against this tendency. Avoid coldness and austerity. Cultivate sympathy and grace. Get outside yourself. Extend your interests. Struggle against every tendency to coldness and pride.

In love you may sometimes be considered too practical and lacking in sentiment; but at heart you are a jealous and exacting lover strongly swayed by your emotions.

Your planetary colors are yellow, yellow-brown, gold, orange, green, ash-gray, maroon, dark brown and black; your flowers, the flax, the holly and the poppy; your stones, the chrysolite, the lodestone, the garnet and all unpolished blue or black gems.

Like most people born under Capricorn, you will be happiest when working hardest. You have great practical gifts.

Use them. Your energy and perseverance, if properly applied, will win success in almost any constructive endeavor where hard work is a main requisite: building, manufacturing, mining, farming.

Saturn, the ruling planet of your sign and the most influential factor in determining your choice of a profession, favors pursuits like plumbing, undertaking, mining, dealing in coal or lead; in fact, anything where success is won by the sweat of the brow and the strength of the good right arm.

The Sun which was also dominant in the heavens when you were born, on the other hand, shines most brightly on those who sit in high places either in commerce or statecraft. It also favors jewelers and all others who work with precious metals. So you see you have a wide field of interesting and important occupations from which to choose your life work. The main thing is to select the line which is most congenial to you and give to it of your best.

You may find life's struggle hard at times. You may think your own progress discouragingly slow. And perhaps, for the moment, it may be so. Saturn, the great disciplinarian, brings his children through trial to success. His influence, too, is usually on the side of delay. But Saturn has a way of looking after his own.

People born under Capricorn, due to these Saturnine influences, often seem to stand still, but they may simply be resting before the final winning spurt. The goat is not the speediest of animals. But he is one of the surest-footed. He usually reaches his goal.

Capricorn people should avoid sweets or too concentrated foods and drink plenty of water between meals. Children born under Capricorn sometimes suffer from acidosis. You should guard against rheumatic tendencies and digestive upsets. Eat simple foods. Drink plenty of water. Above all, look cheerfully on life.

Banish unreasoning fear. Do and dare. You have in you the elements of great material success. Give those elements full play!

AQUARIUS

THE ELEVENTH SIGN

*"He telleth the number of the stars;
He calleth them all by names."*
—Psalms, CXLVIII, 4.

AQUARIUS

ON the heights above the City of New York there is a temple—a temple of glory. It is called "The Hall of Fame." In it are the statues of the American Immortals, sixty-nine figures which stand out in the roll call of the nation's great. And according to statisticians, approximately eighty per cent of those who have been so honored were born under one sign of the Zodiac, Aquarius.

The reason is obvious—to an astrologer. Aquarius is the out-giving sign. It is symbolized by the Man Pouring Water. Men and women born strongly under the influence of this sign live for humanity. They pour themselves out on the world. And they reap the reward which the world gives to such people—fame.

Aquarius' monopoly of famous men and women is not confined to America. The stars are international! In that greater Hall of Fame, which is the list of the world's immortals, the natives of this sign—that is, people born between January 21st and February 19th—are equally prominent. It is a long list. I will not try to give it all. But this brief selection will give some idea of the part this one sign has played in destiny:

Abraham Lincoln, Thomas A. Edison—how's that for a start?—Elihu Root, Robert Burns, Victor Herbert, Sir Henry Irving, Charles M. Schwab, Adelina Patti, Sinclair Lewis, John Barrymore, Havelock Ellis, John D. Rockefeller, Jr., John Ruskin, Franklin D. Roosevelt, Fritz Kreisler, Lord Byron, Thomas Paine, and Charles Augustus Lindbergh.

As water makes the earth yield abundantly, so does the Aquarian have the ability to stir men's souls and to waken the dormant seed into spiritual activity. Those born under the sign Aquarius are kind-hearted, helpful and gentle; they are happiest when asked for their good offices or their advice, and they are usually good counsellors. It is necessary, however, that they should realise "there is danger in the duty of another" and that we help people most when we help them to help themselves. Aquarians are often taken advantage of through an appeal made to their sympathetic, understanding nature, and they are not always appreciated for the sacrifices they make. They must show discrimination in the selection of their friends and not allow their tolerance to blind them to unworthiness or inferiority.

They are modest and unassuming, and are at first often overlooked. This, however, holds no distress for them, as they delight in the contemplation and study of their fellow-men and the world about them. This trait sometimes makes them a little difficult to approach; in fact, their reserve daunts those who attempt to penetrate their quiet exterior. Their real abilities are often underestimated. As a matter of fact, the awakened Aquarians have splendid intellects and may be the mediums through which lasting benefit will be bestowed upon humanity. It behooves them to take advantage of every opportunity which offers, and to make the most of each moment, as it passes. The undeveloped Aquarius-born are more personal and self-interested.

Aquarians should never take the advice of others against their own intuition or judgment, as some of their greatest mistakes or misfortunes are likely to come through being misguided because of their desire to serve and because they lack confidence in their own spiritual or mental powers.

They are naturally of an equable temper, seldom resenting anything unless it appears to them, after calm consideration, to be petty or unjust. This same mental poise minimizes the power of circumstances over them. It matters little to the Aquarian what his environment is; he is equal to it, whatever it may be. They are determined to develop any plan which they have visioned, and although a thousand things interfere, they hold to their conception until the opportunity opens for its accomplishment.

They are free from prejudice and consider nothing impossible. They accept facts which seem opposed to their theories, however startling; and if, after deliberation, such facts are found to be useful, they incorporate them at once and gain the good obtainable from such addition. They acquire knowledge with little effort, but they may not be blessed with extraordinary memories for names or numbers, while facts never escape them. They are not prone to assert themselves and are often the cause of intense surprise to their friends, in that they are able to solve a situation by some simple adjustment, when they have not seemed to be attentive to what was going on about them.

The aim of the Aquarian nature is humanitarian, universality, impersonality, helpfulness—they continue to pour out upon humanity their flood of love and devotion, instead of concentrating it upon purely personal relations. They plan far-reaching reforms and more work for themselves than they can ever expect to accomplish. They are impulsive by nature and often hinder the results of their plans by this trait. They have logical minds and can deduce effects from causes and causes from effects. If you grant their premise, they can reason you into anything and can always illustrate their contention by most convincing similes. They are inventive and constructive.

Aquarius rules the legs, ankles, teeth and circulation, and sympathetically the heart and throat. The diseases to which Aquarians are subject are such as result from poor circulation and lack of elimination, particularly rheumatism or corrupt blood. Those born under this sign are very active on the mental and spiritual plane, but care little for active sports or bodily exercise. They must guard against physical inertia. Plenty of sleep and fresh air, as well as a simple but nourishing diet, is essential to their well-being. If these people insist on living a sedentary life, they are likely to suffer from constipation which will result in auto-intoxication, if nothing more serious.

The great danger of this sign is infection—and whenever the health is poor or fatigue is felt with too little exertion, or insomnia is suffered from, it would be well to consult a reliable physician and ascertain the cause. The trouble frequently arises from infected teeth or tonsils. Due to poor circulation, the Aquarius-born feels the cold more than the average person, and it is essential that they keep warm, particularly their feet. They should never neglect any abrasions or indications of blood poisoning or live in a malarial atmosphere.

People born under Aquarius are so adaptable and have such an unusual understanding of human nature that they can play a constructive part in almost any department of life. For this reason, they can make a financial success in almost any niche in which Fate seems to place them. Money means very little to them, except as a means to an end, and they often prove more fortunate to others than to themselves. Unless engaged in a profession, they should not be in business for themselves, as they are not shrewd enough. The fact that they are making money is not a sufficient incentive for them to be happy in the commercial world; they must feel that they are helping on humanity or "boosting" those who are discouraged or unfortunate.

The Aquarian character is like a cube of rock among spheres. The ordinary pressure from outside which is sufficient to change the sphere's position, has no effect on the cube. There is no other set of people so controlled from within, so nearly master of themselves, as the Aquarians!

If You Were Born Between January 21st and January 30th—

When you were born, the Sun was in the humanitarian sign Aquarius, symbolized by the Man Pouring Water. The planet Uranus, "God of Invention," rules this sign.

So, if you are a true son or daughter of Aquarius, you are essentially a humanitarian. You "pour out." You see things from the cosmic standpoint. You feel a universal rather than a personal love. You are apt to be much more enamored of a school or a hospital or a science than of an individual. In short, you broadcast your affections.

You make friends slowly; but loyalty is one of your strongest traits. The mental and spiritual dominate over the physical and materialistic in your development. You should have almost endless patience, great concentration and a serene mental poise when you have gained self-control. This mental poise is one of your finest characteristics.

If you are a woman, you insist on meeting men on an equal basis, and your mentality entitles you to do so, but this trait does not make a hit with some types of masculinity. However, you have an easy, graceful manner, which should make you popular with both sexes. You have in you the makings of a devoted wife and mother, although your tendency to broadcast your affections instead of concentrating them may cause your loyalty and devotion to be underestimated.

Your planetary colors are light blue, bluish green and ultramarine violet; your flowers, the tulip, the pansy and the daffodil; your stones, the opal, the sapphire, the beryl, the green jasper, the lapis-lazuli and the carnelian. If these colors, flowers and jewels do not become you, you do not need to wear them; but if you do, you will have the satisfaction of knowing that you are dressing in harmony with your stars.

On the physical side, you should be careful of poor circulation, gout, cramps, and rheumatism. You should stimulate elimination and avoid chills. You should take the best possible care of your feet and legs.

Uranus, the ruling planet of your sign and the most influential factor in determining your choice of a profession, governs lecturers, public officials, engineers, mechanics, and all those who follow uncommon pursuits; for example, astrologers, psychologists and metaphysicians.

Venus, which was also dominant in the heavens at the particular time you were born, on the other hand, rules musicians, poets, actors, painters, artists of all kinds; dealers in perfumes, flowers, ornaments and toilet accessories; silk merchants, embroiderers, makers of hats, gloves and women's apparel; clothiers, fancy goods dealers, bakers and confectioners.

Venus will also give you success in the lighter sciences and the fine arts. All Aquarians tend to succeed as teachers, physicians, social workers—anything which involves helpfulness to others—but you, with your special Venus advantages, might do well as a writer, a decorative artist or a public entertainer.

But whatever you do in life, your greatest joy will be to help others, and your greatest danger will be that you may put too much trust in human nature. But you are essentially tenacious. Once you have made up your mind that a thing is right, you do it. And this quality should pull you through all vicissitudes to success!

If You Were Born Between January 31st and February 9th—

You were born in one of the best signs of the Zodiac—and in one of the best parts of that sign. You are what astrology calls an Aquarian child. Mercury, the planet which rules the intellect, was dominant in the heavens when you were born.

All people born under Aquarius are naturally of a humanitarian nature. Their great pleasure is to do good to others. They see the world whole. And they rise above personal desires and selfish aims. You are like that. But because of the special influence of Mercury, you, more than most people, have the power to make use of these traits to the best advantage.

Your planetary colors are blue, bluish green and black; your flowers, the primrose, the pansy and the daffodil; your stones, the agate, the marcasite, the emerald, the topaz, the opal and the sapphire. If these colors, flowers and jewels do not become you, you do not need to wear them; but if you do, you will have the satisfaction of knowing that you are dressing in harmony with your stars.

In love affairs you are essentially loyal and devoted, but inclined to be undemonstrative. You are so interested in the world in general that you may seem to neglect the person you love. Aquarian women should guard especially against this tendency. Men like to feel that they come first in the mind and heart of the woman they love. So, even if you know that you care more about mankind than you do about any individual man, I advise you to keep the fact to yourself.

Uranus, which is the governing planet of your sign, and the most influential factor in determining your choice of a profession, rules the entire field of metaphysics. It also exerts a favorable influence on lecturers, public officials, trav-

elers, electricians and dealers in all kinds of scientific mechanism.

Mercury, on the other hand, governs writers, teachers,
booksellers, printers, accountants, interpreters, registrars,
clerks and letter carriers. You should excel not only as a
physician, teacher, social worker, or inventor, but you may
even become interested in astronomy, astrology, and occult
research.

You do not need to be warned against sloth or changefulness. You work hard and to the end. Your success is won
that way. It is not the over-night kind. It comes slowly,
but it lasts. Eighty per cent of the people in the Hall of
Fame were born under your sign.

You value money not for itself but for the good it will do.
Your greatest reward—and one you will surely get if you
are true to your sign—is the knowledge that you have helped
others to get more out of life.

You are unusually endowed in mind and body. You
possess an intuition which is akin to prophecy. In fact, it is
often taken for prophecy. Your health is generally good.
If properly guarded, there is small chance of serious impairment; but take plenty of exercise and keep the organs func-
tioning freely. Regulate your diet so as to avoid rheumatic
tendencies.

You will always enjoy a good reputation—and deservedly.
You are essentially loyal. Your devotion, once given, knows
no limit in service. Your chief danger is that you may over-
tax yourself in your effort to give too much. Don't forget
that you must save your strength for the world's work.

*If You Were Born Between February 10th and February
19th—*

You were born under Aquarius, the sign of the Zodiac
which is sometimes called the sign of the optimist. But the

natural cheerfulness of your disposition is apt to be clouded, if you don't watch out, by the influence of the Moon, which was dominant in the heavens at the time you were born.

If you are a true son or daughter of your sign—if you are a true Aquarian—you will keep your mind off any troubles which you think you may have and concentrate on what is the chief purpose of people born under this sign: helpfulness to others.

You must not become weary of well-doing or feel discouraged when you suffer from ingratitude, as you must realize that your service is to humanity. Your compensation will come from unexpected sources, rather than directly from those whom you benefit. You rarely, if ever, become depressed or discouraged on account of your own affairs, but you are frequently very sad over the seeming hopelessness of human nature.

Your planetary colors are blue, bluish green, pale yellow, pale green and white; your flowers, the pansy and the daffodil; your stones, the crystal, the moonstone, the opal and the sapphire.

You will best succeed, as all people born under Aquarius do, in some profession which is consecrated to the service of humanity: the practice of medicine, social service, inventing and promoting large philanthropic enterprises.

Uranus, the ruling planet of your sign and the most influential factor in determining your choice of a profession, governs the whole field of metaphysics: astrology, psychology and all that sort of thing. It rules inventors, engineers, public officials, lecturers, electricians and dealers in scientific mechanism.

The Moon, on the other hand, favors those who follow the sea as a profession, either as sailing men or shipping merchants. You should do well in the importing or exporting business. Many people born strongly under the Moon have succeeded as dealers in liquids.

The strong position of the Moon in your horoscope may also lead you to travel much in foreign lands, but you mustn't let your love of travel keep you too long away from home and your real work in life.   Guard against bizarre tastes and fantastic appetites, also against a tendency toward solitude. Learn to be a good mixer.   Force yourself into activity outside of yourself.   Turn your energies into broad channels. This is no reason why you should not make a loyal mate and a successful parent, but your abilities in these lines may not be so obvious to the opposite sex as you might wish.   If you are in love with anyone, concentrate on making him or her feel it.   Above all, cling to the high principles of your sign: loyalty, humanitarian impulses, helpfulness to others.   Don't let the melancholy Moon keep you from realizing the high possibilities which the sign Aquarius and its ruling planet Uranus open up to you.   Pour yourself out.   Give your inventive powers full play.   You will get your reward through useful self-expression!

PISCES

THE TWELFTH SIGN

*"To be or not to be,
That is the question."*
—Shakespeare.

PISCES

FEBRUARY 20TH THROUGH MARCH 21ST

To say that you are a fish is one thing. To say that you are two fishes is two things. And to say that one of you is swimming up stream and the other down is still another thing. In short, it is Pisces!

By Pisces I mean the twelfth and last sign of the Zodiac, which rules the period beginning February 20th and ending March 21st. If your birthday falls in that part of the year you are a Pisces person, and as such you are under the Pisces symbol. And the Pisces symbol, as you probably know, is two fishes swimming in opposite directions.

Pisces people delight in the picturesque in nature and prefer sunshine to shadow. They are honest in intent and seldom expect to find dishonesty. They are prone to accept with perfect confidence what is told them, and have no thought but that it is correct. They are generous to a fault, giving even the necessities for a relative or friend, and asking not for an accounting. They are lovers of beauty in nature and art, seeing first the good and avoiding the bad as far as possible.

Pisces people often deplete themselves by giving out too much in their desire to help others. Unlike the Aquarian, they give both wisely and unwisely, and often impoverish themselves for others, and are annoyed that they cannot give more. They do not suffer from ingratitude, as they do not demand or even deem it necessary that a like return be made. They do, however, express a great deal of their loquaciousness and fussiness through talking about the things they have

137

done for others and enjoy being the martyr; they must guard against falling into the habit of feeling terribly sorry for themselves. They are often selfishly unselfish and unconsciously cause others annoyance by their insistence in giving their time and strength when it is really unwelcome. They are naturally honest and clear, and walk always by preference in clean paths. They delight in assuming responsibility and can usually be depended upon.

They are in no sense egotists; in fact, they are peculiarly lacking in self-esteem. This trait often causes them to feel that they are of little consequence and hence they see no reason for, or make no effort to keep their place in the world. They are not always, but sometimes, "quitters." They are sincerely religious, but not at all "churchy." In everything they are true to the spirit of the law, but not always the letter. They are modest and retiring, but at the same time their nervousness and enthusiasm often makes them conspicuous in their undirected activity. They are inclined to exaggerate their worries, and given to anxiety over things not worth while. They should not expect that unpleasant things and accidents are likely to happen, otherwise they will work themselves into nervous debility by a too active fancy.

They are either over-hopeful, for the time being not recognizing any obstacles, or realizing the time necessary in order to accomplish a task, or they anticipate complete failure if everything does not go just as they expected from the beginning.

Because of their absent-mindedness or inattentiveness, they lose their possessions very easily and are constantly dropping things and forgetting to pick them up. They are so impressionable and intuitive that they lack logic and consistency; for this reason they can at times be very trying and stubborn. They seldom hold steadfastly to any idea and are "blown about by every wind that blows," provided the contrary and stubborn side of their nature is not aroused.

When the Pisces people have recognized and overcome their inherent weaknesses, they become the very salt of the earth—they are then delightful companions, are lovers of their kind, and can become of the greatest use in the world.

It very largely depends upon the people with whom those born under this sign are associated, as to whether they are good talkers with the ability to fall into a conversation and to appear to know more about it than is actually the case, or whether they have nothing to say. They either have too much confidence in people, being too frank and too talkative but if once deceived they are then suspicious and secretive. They gather knowledge subconsciously and often utter truths or even state facts that they have not reasoned out. At one time they are brilliant, cheerful and witty, at another, mentally inactive, with a tendency to be peevish and even melancholy. While Pisces is a very intuitive and inspirational sign, it also endows one with much common sense. If obliged for any length of time to associate with those who are too materialistic or too worldly, they become very discontented and unhappy, and in time this would affect their whole being.

Few people really touch the love nature deeply of the Pisces-born, although they are capable of great devotion and much self-sacrifice and are charitable even to their enemies. Their greatest cross in life is likely to come through their affections, since, when the grand test comes, they may not find others willing to make sacrifices or to do for them what they would be glad to do under the same circumstances. Indeed, they must not be surprised if they find their friends generally rather selfish, as their own selflessness will be rather taken for granted and not always appreciated. They should try to cultivate a little more subtlety in the expression of their affections, and be less demonstrative towards those they wish to fascinate.

The Pisces-born, as a rule, have a strong sense of the ridiculous and can see a funny situation, even at the expense of hurting the feelings of their close associates and best friends. For this reason they may often be considered hypocrites, when in reality they are merely indulging this side of their nature, and with no intent to hurt. Even though their intention may not be unkindly, they must realize that the other person does not understand their motive and is therefore warranted in being hurt. They are often misjudged and mistrusted for this and other reasons.

Like the fish which are seldom quiescent, they are "on the go." Their desire for locomotion may not always exhibit itself in walking, but often in a peculiar fussiness, inability to keep the feet still and inattentiveness to what is being said. Though calm outwardly, they are, in reality, all of a tremor within.

Pisces people work better, so far as business is concerned, in double harness than they do in single. They are so overconscientious and so frequently lacking in self-confidence, that they are rarely successful when in business for themselves. They would do well to connect themselves with some large enterprise or have as a partner someone who would supply the more strenuous qualities necessary to worldly success. When well-developed and finely educated, they make good writers and good painters, and in their work display the clear, clean, bright side of life. Pisces women make devoted wives and unselfish mothers; but they are inclined to be rather casual housekeepers and too indulgent with their children. They should strive to be more methodical and more orderly. Pisces women make good workers among the sick.

Don't be discouraged because I point out the dangers to

which the natives of your sign are exposed. Many able and delightful Pisces people have either conquered or avoided them. In fact, the history of the world has been marked by a long procession of Pisces men and women, each famous in his line, each possessing in some degree their sign's rare and valued gifts. George Washington was born in Pisces. So was Michael Angelo. So were Grover Cleveland, Victor Hugo, William Jennings Bryan, William Dean Howells, Mary Garden, Margaret Deland, Geraldine Farrar, Dr. Eliot of Harvard, and Enrico Caruso.

You, too, can be a Pisces success!

If You Were Born Between February 20th and February 29th—

You were born under the astrological sign Pisces, sometimes called the birth sign of poets, artists and dreamers. The inspirational planet Neptune rules this sign. Pisces is symbolized by two fishes—one swimming upstream and one swimming downstream—and in these opposite forces lie the beauty and the danger of your sign.

You are blessed with naturally good health, but you should protect yourself against colds. They might lead to trouble in the chest or abdomen. Pisces men should keep away from alcoholic drinks, drugs, self-indulgence of any kind. Such things are sometimes a weakness of this sign, and should be avoided.

You should do very well in any line having to do with liquids. You also have capabilities as a teacher or social worker. Neptune, the ruling planet of your sign and the most influential factor in your choice of a profession, favors all those engaged in artistic, æsthetic and inspirational pursuits. It rules the stage and the motion picture industry. It is favorable to writers, especially of the imaginative type.

You have a strongly developed spiritual side to your nature, but you mustn't let your religious tendencies run into fanaticism. The planet Saturn was dominant in the heavens at the time you were born, and people born under this planet sometimes carry enthusiasm into morbidity. Protect your reputation against attacks from false friends or powerful enemies. Avoid quarrels. Concentrate on the best that is in you.

Saturn's influence, by the way, may open up to you other and more strictly practical fields of successful labor; for Saturn governs miners, coal merchants, plumbers and real estate dealers. So you see you have a wide field from which to choose your occupation in life. The main thing is to find something which is congenial to you, and give to it the best you have.

If you are a woman, your love of change may make you loath to settle down to the job of making a home and raising a family, but once you overcome the restlessness of your sign, you become exceedingly fond of domestic life. You should make an understanding mate and a delightful companion.

Your planetary colors are blue, violet and gray; your flowers, mignonette, jessamine and yarrow; your stones, the pearl, the chrysolite, the moonstone, the lodestone, and all unpolished blue and black gems. If these colors, flowers and jewels do not become you, you do not need to wear them; but if you do, you will have the satisfaction of knowing that you are dressing in harmony with your stars.

If you are a true son or daughter of Pisces, you have excellent intuition but you lack confidence. You should have more faith in your insight into the future, which is considerable. You should convince yourself of your ability to do anything you start out to do—then, do it!

If You Were Born Between March 1st and March 9th—

You were fortunate in having the planet Jupiter dominant in the heavens at the time you were born. You should have a warm, sympathetic, genial nature. You should attract powerful friends in high places. You should achieve position and wealth. You are a true child of Jupiter.

But you must not forget that you are also a child of Neptune, which rules the sign of the Zodiac in which you were born. Neptune confers many favors, too, but they are chiefly of the æsthetic and artistic type. A person strongly under the influence of Neptune is highly emotional, given to great enthusiasms, and—like most emotional, enthusiastic persons—capable of dangerous self-deception.

Avoid intrigues and secret alliances. Do not allow yourself to be over-influenced by others. Do not be swerved from your path. Pisces, the astrological sign under which you were born, is symbolized by the two fishes, one swimming up the river and one swimming down. Make sure which way you are going—and don't give up either to the current or the tide.

Your planetary colors are sea-green, blue, purple and violet-red; your flowers, mignonette, jessamine, and yarrow; your stones, the amethyst, the emerald, the sapphire and the pearl. If these colors, flowers and jewels do not become you, you do not need to wear them; but if you do, you will have the satisfaction of knowing that you are dressing in harmony with your stars.

You should have no difficulty, with your favoring Jupiter influences, in learning to concentrate—one of the prime requisites of people in your sign. You will be wise enough to know what some people never learn: that all life is a process of elimination. And you will go about your special task of eliminating what is petty and unimportant in your life.

Preserve your naturally excellent health. Keep away from liquor and all forms of self-indulgence. They are not for you. Be careful about colds: keep them from affecting your chest or your intestines. Get plenty of fresh air. Conserve your energy.

Pisces people usually prosper in the shipping business or any other activity connected with the water. They also make good teachers and religious or social workers.

Neptune, the ruling planet of your sign, and the most influential factor in determining your choice of profession, governs the whole field of artistic, æsthetic and inspirational pursuits. It rules the stage and the motion picture industry. It is friendly to fiction writers and to all others in whom there burns the divine spark of genius. If you have any special talent of an artistic nature, do not hesitate to develop it.

On the other hand, with your Jupiter influence, you ought to succeed in almost any line of endeavor which proves congenial to you. Jupiter casts its rays with special favor on judges, clergymen, lawyers, physicians, bankers and all those active in large affairs.

So, although your natural tendencies may lead you along inspirational Neptunian lines, the practical, wealth-giving Jupiter will always be ready with opportunities of quite another sort!

If You Were Born Between March 10th and March 21st—

You were born under Pisces, an astrological sign which makes you sensitive, sympathetic, intuitive and agreeable. You make an excellent companion; and you should make a pleasing, comfortable, lovable husband or wife. You have high ideals and fine feelings. You are interested, or should be, in all artistic and æsthetic things.

Many of the natives of your sign are natural wanderers and lack concentration and directness. They are restless physically and inattentive mentally. They should not have too many conflicting interests, and should strive to overcome a tendency to scatter their forces. They often ask needless questions and seldom wait for a reply. Most people ask questions because they desire information, but the Pisces people do so merely to give vent to their feelings of the moment.

You should be careful to allow no disorganizing elements to deter you from realizing your full possibilities. This warning applies to love as well as business. Your naturally demonstrative nature may be rebuffed by an apparent failure to respond on the part of the person you love. Pisces women especially have to learn that man should be the lover, woman the loved.

Your planetary colors are blood-red, violet-red, scarlet, mauve and lavender; your flowers, mignonette, jessamine and yarrow; your stones, the moonstone, the crystal and the pearl.

The powerful planet Mars was dominant in the heavens when you were born. This fact does not mean that you will necessarily be quarrelsome and warlike. Mars gives his sons and daughters courage, energy, strength—and your task is to mobilize these forces against its less helpful qualities. Avoid strifes and enmities. Be brave without being rash. Eschew fanciful projects. Try to keep your domestic life tranquil. Concentrate on the best in life.

But the inspirational planet Neptune, which rules the sign Pisces, is an even more influential factor in your life. Neptune makes for enjoyment of poetry and art; but it also denotes uncertainty, camouflage, a tendency to self-deception, susceptibility to influence—especially from the opposite sex. Do not let the combination of Neptune's emotionalism and Mars' passionate nature divert you from your true self.

Mars rules soldiers, surgeons, dentists, chemists, barbers, workers in iron and steel. On the other hand, Neptune favors artists, writers, and all people who work with the imagination. It rules the stage and the motion picture industry. Under the influence of this powerful planet you may find yourself successfully engaged in almost any pursuit of an æsthetic or inspirational nature.

In business, play safe. Make powerful friends. Protect yourself against sudden reversals. Do not go into strange, untried enterprises. You should succeed in foreign commerce, shipping—in fact, anything which has to do with the water, including the navy.

Be careful physically, too. Take care of your lungs and your intestinal tract. Avoid colds. Get plenty of exercise. And don't drink!

THE PLANETS

*"Ye stars which are the poetry of heaven!
If in your bright leaves we would read the fate
of men and empires—'tis to be forgiven."*
— Lord Byron.

THE SUN

"GIVER OF LIFE"

THE Sun is sometimes called "The Father of the Stars."
And in a strictly scientific sense, this is a fairly accurate
definition. For in astrology as in nature, the Sun is the
center and giver of all life and strength—the parent of the
entire solar system.

It is so important a factor in determining our individuality that there has been built around its influence a science
of its own, often confused with astrology, called Solar Biology. From one viewpoint, Solar Biology is merely a poor
relation to the greater science; but from another viewpoint,
it is the basis and foundation stone.

When an astrologer says that you are a Sagittarius child
or a Capricorn child or a Gemini child or a Leo child, what
he or she really means is that the Sun was in that sign at
the moment you were born. From this one fact—without
regard to the position of the Moon and the other planets—
it is possible to tell a great deal about a person's character
and about his destiny in so far as character is destiny. That
is why these so-called astrology books that are read as parlor
games and these horoscopes which appear in the newspapers
are so often astonishingly correct even though our common
sense tells us that they must apply to everyone born within
a period of nearly thirty days and cannot be absolutely true
of all of them.

It cannot be too clearly understood that in astrology as
in nature, the Sun is the pivot around which our world
revolves.

The Sun governs the back, the heart and the arteries. His diseases, such as palpitation of the heart, weak eye-sight and ailments of the arterial system, are organic troubles rather than functional disorders. The Sun's metal is gold; his colors are yellow, orange, brown and gold; his precious stones are the diamond and the ruby. He bestows honors, glory, fame, public office, health and power. He renders those born under his influence honest, free, generous, ambitious, noble, wise. His influence is electric, vital, fiery. His goal is the highest fulfillment of life.

The Sun is the ruling planet of the royal sign Leo, and may, therefore, be said to govern all those born between July 24th and August 23rd. If your birthday falls during this period you are unusually favored by the Sun's life-giving influence. The Sun is also especially influential in the lives of people born under Aries during the first ten days of April, in which time the Sun attains what we astrologers call its "exaltations." It is also a particularly dominating factor in the lives of people born June 12th to June 22nd, or in the last week of August, or in the first ten days of November, or from January 11th to January 21st—which are, roughly speaking, the "decans" over which the Sun has special dominion.

If you were born at any of these times you may consider yourself, at least in part, a child of the Sun, or, as we astrologers say, a "native" of the Sun.

Where the Sun is a dominant influence in the life, the will is strong and the character masterful, and the confidence given by self-respect and a cheerful outlook toward life will cause the native to attract much good fortune. He may find it necessary to guard against being too frank and outspoken and to cultivate caution and secretiveness. He must not allow his fondness of display to encourage the "exhibition complex." He is qualified to look into the mysteries of life, to make a study of nature's finer forces, and is given the power to rise above the station to which he is born; others will just naturally turn to him for counsel and assistance.

Many holding government positions or those of a purely executive character are born strongly under the influence of this luminary, and it all depends on one's sphere as to the degree and type of success attained.

The Sun represents the constitution, the life principle, and the character. Where the Sun is strong, it does not, of itself, imply more than the vigor of powerful animal life, which enables the native to reap the rewards of favorable planetary aspects and, conversely, to suffer and endure the buffets of adverse influences. Where the Sun is weak, no amount of benefits from the other planets will counteract that affliction.

A moment's reflection will disclose the soundness of this proposition, since it is evident that no matter what capacity a man may possess, he will not be able to employ it profitably if his life is too short for him to develop it or too broken by spells of illness for him to prosecute it with that continuity which is necessary to success.

So, if you were born at any of the times when the Sun is especially powerful, or if the Sun is in a favorable position in your chart, you are to be congratulated. As a true child of the Sun, you should be ambitious and a tireless worker. You should have a magnetic quality, and should see *in person* anyone whom you desire to influence.

Naturally, with such strong virtues there are also some dangers. You should curb your desire to rule others, lest you appear too dominating and defeat your own purpose. You should not allow your ambition to make you discontented or unhappy. Don't yield to the desire to show off. Discount all flattery fifty per cent, and take the balance with a grain of salt. You should develop your higher mental side, and make a special effort to avoid being domineering.

You are capable of the highest devotion to those you love—of an adoration which amounts to worship. You may be hurt by the inability of some people to respond in either kind or degree; but, on the other hand, the generosity and abandon of your love may rouse the same qualities and give you the response which your warm, affectionate nature craves. You have the power to win great victories in the field of love. Do not be overbearing. Do not demand the center of the stage. Show your man—or your woman—the warmth of your disposition rather than its aggressiveness.

THE MOON

"RULER OF THE SENSES"

THE Moon, which is the most rapidly moving of all the heavenly bodies, governs daily happenings. If the Moon is in Capricorn, the day takes on the aspects of the sign Capricorn, which, applied to a day, aren't as good as they might be. If the Moon is in Aquarius, the day will take on the aspects of the sign Aquarius, which makes it a very good day *indeed*. That is the way it works; and that is why the Moon is one heavenly body about which we should learn all we can.

Moreover, the Moon does not confine its influence to the character of the days through which we must live. It affects in a very vital way the personality just as the Sun rules the individuality. Perhaps it would be better to say that the Moon typifies our personality in much the same way that the Sun typifies our character. The Moon is not the positive force that the Sun is. It performs the offices of a conductor of power rather than of a generator. It is the medium through which life's forces flow, the lens through which our consciousness receives the manifestations of the external world. In a large, fundamental way, the Sun is masculine, and the Moon is feminine.

Each planet—and by planet I include both the Sun and the Moon, although neither is a planet in the strict dictionary sense—in addition to its basic influence and purpose, performs other duties in the celestial household; and the Moon, being feminine, performs a good many of them! The Moon rules travel and travelers, the sea and all those who go down

153

to it in ships. It rules liquids and all those engaged in their sale or manufacture. It rules the masses, as distinguished from the classes, and all those who cater to them or profit by them. It rules feminine influences and relations as distinguished from sex influences and sex relations—for example, the mother, the sister, the woman friend, and the wife as a companion rather than as a lover. And it rules particularly the domestic sign Cancer, whose dominant planet it is.

If you were born between June 22nd and July 23rd, you are a Cancer child, and are strongly under the influence of the Moon. If you were born in the first ten days of May, or the last week in September, or the first ten days of December, or from February 10th to February 19th, you are also strongly under the influence of the Moon, but not in the same degree that you would have been if you had been born under the Moon's sign, Cancer.

What the effect of the Moon may be on those born strongly under its influence depends largely on where the other planets were in relation to it when the individual was born. The Moon, being negative in its own force, takes on the forces of others. It is the most impressionable of the heavenly bodies and the most changeable, and for this reason its influence is often most unsettling. It gives the desire to change one's occupation or place of residence too frequently, or it may simply prompt the frequent moving of furniture and rearrangement of the home.

The Moon is also influenced—more acutely than any of the other planets—by the sign in which it happens to be. For example: When the Moon is in Aries, I cannot recommend starting on a journey or for that matter starting anything at all which you may wish to have go smoothly to a successful conclusion. Of course, you can go on a journey on an Aries day. There is nothing sinister about it. But the chances are that you will change your itinerary more than once before you come once again into the same port. The same way with other undertakings; they may come out all right, but the chances are that they will be pretty much up in the air—*and you along with them!*

If you happen to have the Moon in Aries in your individual chart—I use Aries as an example only because it is the first of the twelve signs of the Zodiac—you need not despair. There are many compensations. People born with the Moon in Aries are very apt to have power over multitudes. Among modern politicians, Gifford Pinchot is such a man. And I could give you many others who have been successful through their pens or their voices in swaying large numbers of people. For example: Robespierre, Northcliffe, Oliver Wendell Holmes, whose essays and poetry gained wide popularity when some of us were younger; Emile Coué, whose "better-and-better" formula swept across the world like an epidemic of optimism; Harriet Beecher Stowe, whose "Uncle Tom's Cabin" was the most influential book of its time; Henry George, whose single tax ideas shook the foundations of American political economy; Booth Tarkington, one of the most widely read novelists of modern times; and a long list of famous actors and actresses, including John Drew, E. H. Sothern, and our beloved Maude Adams.

It must be obvious, from these examples, that the Moon is a very important factor in human life. Take Madame Ganna Walska, wife of Harold McCormick, the Chicago millionaire. Madame Walska has won great success through her marriage, but has met with repeated rebuffs in her attempts to scale the operatic heights. The obvious reason— at least it is obvious to an astrologer—is that her Moon is in Leo in conjunction with Venus and friendly to Mars, which gives her unusual personal magnetism, instead of in Taurus, which rules the throat. Taurus is one of the best signs in which the Moon can be found. Many people who have appealed to a wide public had it so placed. Shakespeare did; and Queen Elizabeth, and those widely differing religious leaders, Swedenborg and St. John.

The effect of the Moon on our daily lives depends also on the size and condition. When the new Moon comes into being, all Nature begins to renew itself; even you and I begin to gather new powers. It is Nature's way. From the New Moon up to the Full, she is giving out her strength, and we are waxing strong with it; from the Full Moon to the end, she is withdrawing her strength preparatory to giving it out again, and we are waning in our own powers because of this withdrawal. It is a well-known fact, recognized by merchants, that no one does anything during the last days of the Old Moon that they can possibly put off until the first days of the new one. R. H. White, the great Boston department store owner, once told me that the floors of his store were practically deserted during this period.

Everything slows down on the last days of the Moon—not only people, but animals and everything else in Nature. I had a member of a famous Chicago packer's family as a client for some years, and I asked him once if he had found it true in his business, as the ancient astrologers had always maintained, that hogs killed in the last days of the Old Moon invariably shrank and produced less meat. He said that he certainly had found it to be so, and that, although the necessity of keeping his plants in operation forced him to go right on killing, he never expected to get so much meat out of a carload of hogs killed during the last days of the Old Moon as at any other time. So it is with man-meat, and man-energy, and man-power to accomplish things. It shrinks.

The ancient astrologers called this "shrinking" period, "the Moon of the Black Magician." Of course, modern astrologers, like other modern scientists, do not believe in magic, either white or black; they do not believe that some wicked genii are working their machinations "on the dark of the Moon"; but they do believe in the inevitable effects of natural law, and they advise their followers accordingly.

Therefore, I advise you to waste no time, when the Moon is in its last days, starting new enterprises or doing unusual things. Save up your bright ideas for the coming of the New Moon, when all Nature will be brighter, too; when everybody you meet will be more anxious to cooperate with you, when the chances of your success will be increased a hundredfold!

MERCURY

"MESSENGER OF THE GODS"

NEXT to the Sun and the Moon, Mercury is the most important heavenly body in determining the horoscope, because it increases the influences of the other planets for either "good" or "bad."

Naturally, people born strongly under the influence of such a mercurial planet are especially subject to moods. I remember the case of a grand opera singer of international fame who came in to see me to ask if she should get rid of her devoted but no longer thrilling husband. I read the diva's horoscope and discovered that she was subject to these "Mercury moods," often without cause, and that when she was in the "dip" of one of these slumps, she was apt to do foolish things.

"That's extraordinary," agreed the singer. "What you say has always been true of me."

"Wait until the mood passes," I counselled. "You are coming under better conditions presently, and your husband is coming into the best period he has had in twenty-one years."

The singer was about to sail for Europe to get her divorce in Paris. I did not know at the time whether my words had any effect. But that night, as I was leaving my studio, a messenger arrived from the Metropolitan Opera House, carrying a huge box of American beauties and this note:

"Dear Miss Adams: I have decided to take the wiser part. I am sailing tomorrow *with* my husband."

158

The only trouble is: I cannot get hold of all you Mercury people in time!

But, of course, not all the sons and daughters of Mercury want to get divorces. Some of them are using the energy of their dominant planet in more constructive ways. For Mercury exercises dominion over the mind and all mental things. It favors writers, editors, publishers, printers, booksellers, and all others connected with the production and distribution of literature. It also favors research workers, teachers and accountants.

It is especially influential in the lives of all people born under Gemini between May 22nd and June 21st or under Virgo between August 24th and September 23rd, because it is the ruling planet of both of these highly mental signs. In only slightly lesser degree does it affect those people born in the last ten days of April, the first ten days in July, the last ten days of November, and the first ten days of February.

Variety is the breath of life to these people, particularly those born under Gemini. They would do well to force themselves to finish the various undertakings they start before taking up an entirely new set. They are so versatile they often find it necessary to guard against scattering their forces, and should practice concentration.

Lack of decision is one of their greatest faults and drawbacks to happiness and success. They are constantly torn between two courses of action, as to whether they should go here or there, do this or that—and after having made a decision, they still wonder whether it would not have been better to have done the other thing.

They should cultivate will power. Also, they should be less influenced by the people with whom they are thrown and less dependent upon environment. They should make their own decisions and then stick to them. It is only through the lessons they gain from experience that they will build character and rise above their tendency to go to extremes in mood.

It is most necessary that they should have a purpose in life, as they are inclined to do things for the joy of doing them, rather than for results. Their insatiable mental curiosity moves them to many unwise actions. The fact that their motives are prompted by a desire to ascertain the reactions produced on the undeveloped mind, the conservative mind and the sophisticated mind, does not keep them from being misunderstood or criticised. It would be well for them to realize that it is quite as necessary to avoid the appearances of evil as evil itself.

Mercury is the most truly sensitive of all planets. Venus and the Moon are more easily affected, it is true, but for them a better term is "impressionable." Mercury responds to every impression as does the weather vane, which is a very different thing from the receipt and reflection of every impression. Mercury is not modified by the signs as are the more passive planets; rather, each excites him to some new expression. It has been well said that thousands of people before Newton saw apples fall from trees, but their only impulse was to eat them.

Mercury in the thermometer rises and falls according to temperature, but it is still Mercury; and so it is in astrology: whatever aspects may exist at a given time will not alter the essential character of the planet. Such impressions as are made on Mercury are not like seals upon wax, but like the rise and fall of the column of quicksilver at every change in the atmosphere.

The desire for knowledge, the longing for change, and the cosmopolitan spirit of those born strongly under this planet will cause them to feel the wanderlust, and consequently to take many journeys and make many changes. Their keen intuition and ability to sense what people are about to say often causes them to interrupt in conversation and to change the subject so quickly that at times it is difficult to follow them.

It will all depend on their environment and mental development whether their inquisitive nature will cause them to be curious over petty things or those of more importance. They should realize that their restiveness and tendency to be too easily bored is caused by their own mercurial nature and is not the fault of people or circumstances. Lack of decision and a tendency to allow the attention to wander are two of their outstanding characteristics, which may prevent their permanent success.

The mind of these people is never at rest, and for this reason they require more sleep and fresh air than does the average person. They should guard against being too introspective and should associate as much as possible with spiritually minded people. In the physical body, Mercury governs the brains, nerves, bowels, lungs, tongue, hands, arms, mouth and the whole nervous system. Its influence is active, excitable, changeful and stimulating. Its colors are black, blue, orange and slate-gray. Its stones are the agate, marcasite, emerald and topaz.

If you are a true son or daughter of Mercury, you are above all things "quick on the trigger." Your mind works rapidly and accurately. But you are subject to moods. You are either up or down. You are "mercurial" in every sense of the word. But there are many more good things than bad things about your star of destiny. The aim of every person born under its influence should be to avoid the "bad" and take full advantage of the "good."

The God of the Intellect is a powerful ally to have on your side of life's battle!

VENUS

"GODDESS OF LOVE AND BEAUTY"

I REMEMBER once when I was "breaking in" a new secretary, one of the first duties I assigned to her was to sort the morning mail. When she had completed her task—and, believe me, it *is* a task, for I get letters from every corner of this starlit earth!—she laid a pile of papers on my desk for "immediate attention."

The first letter my eye rested on was from a woman in Texas. It read: "I am anxious to get your address, and you needn't be afraid to send it to me, because I'm a settled woman—nearly 40 years old."

I studied the letter carefully, from the Waco date line to the Spencerian signature. Then, with that confidence which comes from experience, I said:

"This woman wants to know about her Venus."

"Her Venus?" said the newcomer. "How do you know she *has* one?"

"Everybody has a Venus," I explained.

"But how do you know she wants to know about hers?"

"Everybody does!"

And that's the truth! You may laugh at the thought of serious men and women taking up my time and theirs, trying to find out whereabouts in the astrological heavens the Goddess of Love happened to be at the moment of their birth. But you wouldn't laugh if you had heard as many life stories as I have heard during my thirty-five years of horoscope reading!

People may come to my studio in Carnegie Hall to ask

162

me what I think about the war in China, or whether the President's horoscope indicates that we are going to have good times in the fall, or whether September would be an opportune time to produce a play—but they end up, ninety out of every one hundred, talking about love.

And to good purpose!

I can show you among my correspondents in different parts of the world hundreds of happy marriages arranged on the astrological plan. In fact, I am thinking right now of a two-generation example. Years ago a woman came to me who occupied a high social and intellectual position in the community. She was in love with a well-known man, an artist or an author, as I remember it. He was a man of unimpeachable character, but not at all fitted, according to the stars, to mate with the woman who was my consultant. I felt that I was taking a great responsibility, but I insisted that she had not yet found her destiny.

The woman went away, partially convinced. She did not break off the engagement, but she did delay its consummation; not once, but several times; and, in the end, she fell in love with another man, astrologically suited to her, with whom she is still living in the greatest mutual happiness.

Naturally, she and her husband became frequent callers. And, in the course of years, they began to ask me about their daughter's love affairs. She was a most attractive girl, with many suitors. But none of them met my astrological standards; and none of them succeeded—either because of the parents' tact or the girl's own common sense—in persuading her to marry.

Finally, the mother brought me the dates of a young man who had an especially attractive horoscope, complementary to the daughter's in all the vital ways that we have been discussing, and containing promise of a brilliant career—

if not in writing, at least, in something to do with literature. Several years later, the editor of one of our best known magazines entered my studio.

"I've come," he said, "to thank you."

"Thank me?" I replied, puzzled. "Thank me for what?"

"For my wife!"

As a matter of fact, it makes a great deal of difference to all of us, not only what Venus was doing when we were born, but what she does from time to time throughout our lives. For her influence depends, to a great extent, on the sign in which she happens to be, and on her ever-changing position in relation to other planets.

I recall one period especially, when we had a very interesting situation, involving Venus and Mars. The two planets, known in mythology as Psyche and Cupid, were very friendly. This is not an unfavorable vibration. Quite the contrary! It is bound to create a marvelous time for entertaining and being entertained, for having a good time or giving a good time to others, for seeing old friends and meeting new ones, for strengthening old contacts and making new ones—*and for love.*

On the latter point, however, I was forced to give my clients a word of caution, because Venus was at the time in the sign Scorpio, the most strongly sexed of all the signs of the Zodiac and one of the most powerful. This fact, combined with her friendliness to the stimulating and restless Mars, tended to make lovers go to extremes and do things that they would afterward regret. There was one day in particular about which I warned people to be careful. I venture to say there was a bigger business in engagement rings after that day's love-making than jewelers had known in months!

Naturally, these vibrations which enhance our emotional susceptibility affect our judgment on business and financial matters, and make it necessary for us to exercise circumspection in everything we do in those lines. Which brings me to the important astrological fact that Venus is much more than the Goddess of Love. She is the dominant planet in the lives of all people born in the sign Taurus between April 21st and May 21st and in the sign Libra between September 24th and October 23rd. She is also an influential factor in the horoscope of those born between the 11th and the 20th of April, in the last ten days of June, in the first ten days of September, between the 13th and the 22nd of November and in the last ten days of January.

Venus is especially favorable to musicians, painters, poets, actors, artists of all sorts; to makers of toilet accessories, manufacturers of women's apparel, and sellers of articles of personal adornment; to florists, perfumers and confectioners. She is the goddess of entertainment, of parties, of play; she stands for beauty and grace; for art and poetry and music; for good things to eat and good things to wear; for perfume and flowers and jewels; for the niceties of life.

That is why she is called "The Lesser Fortune" as distinguished from Jupiter, "The Greater Fortune," who stands for the bigger things of life; for nobility and wisdom; for power and position; for wealth and glory; for friends, protection, security, happiness in the big, solid sense. From a worldly standpoint Venus presides over the social life; Jupiter over the business life. From a personal standpoint, Venus makes her children gentle, cultured, affectionate, agreeable, gracefully poised, delicately attuned. Jupiter makes his children jovial, generous, sympathetic, noble and wise.

If Venus and Jupiter are both favorable on any given day, that day is a very good time for functions combining business and pleasure. It is a good time for parties generally. You have no idea how many people consult me on this subject—mothers who wish to give parties for their débutante daughters, daughters who wish to choose favorable and sunny days for their weddings, hostesses who wish to give musicales and receptions, anybody and everybody bent on a good time. And theatrical managers consult me as to auspicious nights to put on their new plays.

"The only trouble," Daniel Frohman once said to me, "is that we can't always follow your advice."

That's the hard part about being an astrologer: some people can't follow your advice and some won't! I once told a woman who said that she was going to be married that she shouldn't do it until her conditions were better. Of course, she asked me what would happen if she did.

"I don't know," I answered. "But *something* will—for you are coming under the worst conditions for marriage that you'll be under for twenty-one years."

"What do you mean by that?" she asked.

"I mean there'll be something wrong about your marriage, something impractical or perhaps illegal."

Of course she laughed at me. She had found her beau ideal, and she married him. Two years later, she called again.

"You were right," she said, "about not marrying that man."

"What was the trouble?"

"Nothing much," she smiled grimly, "he was just a bigamist!"

MARS

"THE GOD OF WAR"

WE have already seen that it makes a great deal of difference what sign a planet happens to be in, so far as its effect on our lives is concerned. When Venus is in the impersonal, esthetic sign Libra, our love affairs are apt to be of the gentle, romantic type; when she moves over into Scorpio, they take on a fiercer and more physical character. So it is with Mars. And I think I can best explain the way its changing moods affect our lives by recalling an actual summer period during which Mars was in Taurus and a subsequent autumn during which it was in the radically different signs Cancer and Leo.

When it was in Taurus, there was great danger of people going to excesses in eating and drinking and self-indulgence generally; and there was a consequent danger of accidents and other mishaps due to these excesses. My clients will remember how I warned them against motor accidents on some of those summer week-ends!

When Mars moved over, as it did in the fall, into the sign Cancer, ruling the stomach and intestines, there was danger of digestive upsets and gastric troubles such as flatulence. It also became essential that we refrain from mental irritation lest we aggravate this condition and bring on serious complications.

Moreover, the planets in their course affect us variously not only according to the sign whose color and nature they have for the time being assumed, but according to the dates on which we ourselves were born. For instance, that condition of Mars of which I just spoke—which is likely to cause acidity and flatulence, as well as mental irritation and antagonism—lasted that year through the first twenty days of October. During those days I advised *all* of my clients to choose their food carefully and to keep calm mentally, too; but I was particularly solicitous in regard to those born between January 10th and 21st of any past year, or between April 10th and 21st, or between July 12th and 24th, or between October 13th and 24th.

People born at these times should have been especially careful not only to guard their health, but not to go around with a chip on their shoulders. They should have avoided arguments and quarrels even though they were in the right. That was a hard assignment, wasn't it—especially when Mars, the God of War, was active in the astrological heavens?

In the same way, if you were born between March 25th and 29th of any past year, or during the last five days of June, or during the last four days of September, or between December 26th and 30th, you were also likely during that period to suffer not only in health but in mind, but you could avoid any unfortunate results from this vibration if you strove to keep your equilibrium and refrain from forcing issues, even if your business, domestic or social affairs were contrary to your expectations. "Go with the tide this month," I told these people, *"you might as well, because you won't get anywhere trying to swim against it!"*

Women born during these periods—March 25th to 29th, last five days in June, last four days of September, December 26th to 30th—were apt to feel very tense and nervous, and as a result, they were inclined to push their friends from them and keep good things from coming to them. They were likely to be less magnetic than usual, to have less of what used to be called "come hither" and which I believe is now called "it," so they were obliged to make up for this lack by being tactful and considerate and refusing to harbor resentment. Married women, if they were wise, made very great efforts to "put up with" their husbands; and unmarried women—oh, well, unmarried women usually know what to do!

So much for the effect of Mars on the individual when it was in Cancer. When it moved over into Leo, as it did on the 21st of that particular October, an entirely new set of dangers presented themselves and an entirely new group of people were practically involved.

Leo governs the heart and spinal column and sympathetically the organs of generation, the throat and circulation. All heart affections, spinal meningitis, angina pectoris, aneurism and muscular rheumatism in the back will be easily aggravated during the passage of Mars through Leo, especially if the system becomes depleted, or is susceptible to these ailments.

Mars also affects all of us differently on different days. If you have felt a little more restless and quarrelsome than usual on a certain day, it may not be altogether your fault. It may be Mars, the God of War, stirring things up in the astrological heavens. Perhaps he has been very powerful all day, spreading his aggressive, warlike influence throughout the world; so, if you have come through the day without losing your temper completely or picking a fight with your best friend, you have done well. You may congratulate yourself. For Mars, in such a mood, is hard to control.

You may congratulate yourself, too, if you have come through that kind of day without any serious accident. If Mars can't "get" you mentally, he is apt to try to "get" you physically! A day when Mars is unfriendly is never a good day to pass red lights; but it is a good day to postpone railroad journeys and all unnecessary risks.

Mars has his good side, though. His aggressiveness can

be changed into confidence and initiative and energy and courage. Oliver Cromwell, for instance, had the good qualities of Mars along with his warlike spirit. St. Mark is an even better example. He was one of the most aggressive and enterprising of the Apostles. He went everywhere preaching the word of God: That's the way he earned his title of "The Evangelist." Among living men, the great inventor Marconi is an excellent example of a Martian determination that would not be downed.

So when Mars is in the ascendency, you must not be discouraged. You can, if you will, turn Mars' warlike forces to your own advantage, and to the world's.

Mars always affects with especial force those who were born under Aries (between March 22nd and April 20th) and under Scorpio (between October 24th and November 22nd). It also is extremely influential in the lives of people born during the first ten days of January, from March 12th to 22nd, or during the first ten days of June.

Your problem, if you are a son or daughter of Mars, is to convert your planet's warlike qualities from aggressiveness into ambition, from quarrelsomeness into courage, from destructiveness into constructiveness. If you do, you will come out victorious in the battles of peace as well as of war!

JUPITER

"THE GREATER FORTUNE"

SUCCESS, honor, glory, wealth! That is a large order! But Jupiter, most beneficent of the planets, is quite capable of filling it. That is why Jupiter is called "The Greater Fortune" and "The Eleventh Hour Friend."

The sign in which Jupiter is most powerful is the frank and open Sagittarius; so if you were born between November 23rd and December 22nd, you are particularly favored by this powerful planet. There are certain other brief periods scattered through the year, where Jupiter is almost the most powerful planet, for example: the last ten days of May, the first ten days of August, between October 15th and 24th, and the last ten days of December; and if you were born at any of these times, you are also in line for Jupiter's benefits.

The sign in which Jupiter happens to be from time to time is important, too, not only to Jupiter's own children, but to *all* of us. In addition to the special benefits, which Jupiter bestows on certain people at certain times, there are many departments of life in which Jupiter continually affects us all. For example, it must be obvious, since Jupiter rules both money and success, that it is the planet which has most to say about our jobs: that it is the most important planet, not only in solving the *un*employment problem with which some of us must grapple during hard times, but in solving the *em*ployment problem for *all* of us all of the time.

I have told you before that the planets are the second hands and minute hands and hour hands of the astrological clock. The Moon, for example, is a second hand: it changes from one sign of the Zodiac to another every two or three days. The Sun, on the other hand, passes into a new sign only once a month. And Jupiter, majestic creature that he is, marches slowly through the heavens with a still more leisurely stride, frequently staying in one sign for a year or more at a stretch. It is natural, therefore, that a continuing condition of this sort, especially since it affects so important and powerful a planet, should have a marked influence on all our lives.

So, likewise, do the changes when they come!

For example: during the hard winter of 1930 and 1931, the "hand-to-mouth" buying policy induced by the fact that Jupiter was in the thrifty sign Cancer was undoubtedly responsible in no small measure for the scarcity of jobs. Jupiter in Cancer does favor certain lines: for example, chemists, wholesale merchants, importers and exporters and certain manufacturers (especially those concerned with liquids or with feeding and housing the masses), also nurses, dietitians, and all those concerned with the care of children, the preparation of food and the conduct of the home. Outside of these special lines, however, the beneficent influence of Jupiter while it is in the sign of Cancer is not likely to be felt.

Jupiter in Leo, on the other hand, is favorable to all those at the head of business enterprises and, therefore, to business in general. It particularly favors directors and managers of important enterprises, officers of banks and others occupying positions of authority and trust. Furthermore, Jupiter in this sign inspires in all of us a generous, forward-looking, optimistic, confident attitude toward life which is bound to stimulate buying and, as a result, help to stabilize and improve employment conditions.

We Americans are peculiarly susceptible to that influence which is called "mass psychology." We run with the crowd.

Some critics are even so unkind as to call us "sheep." And because of this national characteristic, we, as a nation, are especially susceptible to Jupiter's changing moods. That is one reason why our stock market goes up with a rush and then goes down with a rush. In fact, it is extraordinary also how quickly not only the business world but the individual responds to the varied aspects of the planet Jupiter. I have told elsewhere about Jupiter and Saturn entering the thrifty sign Virgo in the fall of 1919, and how the period of prodigal spending which had followed the World War halted immediately—and we had the famous "buyers' " strike. Well, the same thing happens in our individual horoscopes, although, unfortunately, it does not always result in such desirable things as thrift.

I had one client, "a big copper and iron man from the West," who first came to me in 1924 to ask about a mine which he had just started to open up. I saw right away that he had undertaken this venture when he was under a most unfortunate affliction of his Jupiter, and that immediate success was out of the question.

"Better shut down," I said, "and wait for more favorable conditions."

But he couldn't do that—or thought he couldn't—because of his associates. So he kept on boring. Pretty soon, the fifty thousand dollars he had appropriated for experimental purposes was used up—and no ore in sight. Then, a hundred thousand, two hundred, *three* hundred without success— until a few months later the unfavorable aspects wore off, and by opening a new shaft and starting all over again, he struck the vein which he had hitherto sought without success. When I last saw him, he expected to make a fortune out of this mine. But the money he spent during those months when his Jupiter was afflicted went for nothing. He might better have taken astrology's advice—and waited.

But Jupiter's influence is not confined to material things. As the symbol of wisdom and the largest planet of our solar system, he naturally exerts a powerful influence over everything. His effect is, however, very much modified by his position with relation to other planets. If Jupiter is in aspect to Mars, he gives tremendous ability, but with more grandeur in the influence than would be the case if in aspect to Saturn, which has a subduing influence and, therefore, restricts optimism and faith.

Three forceful and passionate poets, Shelley, Baudelaire and Swinburne, were born, for example, under a conjunction of Mars and Jupiter. All three are notable for the intensity of their fire. In the religious world, we have Martin Luther. In finance, we had J. P. Morgan, and still have J. D. Rockefeller, as marked examples of the effect of Mars and Jupiter in conjunction. In politics, we have Kruger, who built up the Transvaal Republic so powerfully that it was able to defy the armed might of England—a handful of sixty thousand farmers against four hundred thousand soldiers—for three years. There is also Winston Churchill, one of the most successful politicians that England has produced in the present generation.

In short, Jupiter is not only powerful in himself, but in conjunction with the other planets, he exercises a far-reaching influence on all mankind.

SATURN

"THE CELESTIAL SCHOOLMASTER"

"Cheer up! Things aren't as bad as they seem!"

That is what I am always saying to Saturn's children. And they need it. For Saturn is the gloomy member of the heavenly family. He stands for delay and age and death; for everything that clogs and decays and darkens. His colors are black and indigo. His metal is lead.

That's the kind of planet Saturn is!

So, if you find yourself getting tense and drawn and cross and glum at the end of a day's work, you are probably suffering under a temporary affliction of gloomy old Saturn— and about all you can do about it is to wait until it passes.

Obviously, you should make no attempt to do business at such a time. You should not even try to give a party which combines business with pleasure. In fact, you should not try to give any party at all. Don't call on your "girl." Or, if you are a girl, don't be in to callers! If you are ill, take special precautions to guard against a set-back. If you are well, select your food and your drinks and your pleasure with unusual care so that you won't become ill. Do nothing that you are not obliged to do until Saturn has passed out of your astrological picture, or until it has assumed a more friendly aspect.

For even Saturn is not always bad. Man needs discipline; he needs to be brought down to earth; he needs to be shown how to materialize his talents on a practical plane. And Saturn does all these things. That is why he is called "The Great Disciplinarian," "The Celestial Schoolmaster."

But discipline is seldom a cheerful matter. Neither, for that matter, is school! So it must be admitted that Saturn's influence is, first of all, on the dark side. In my own work, I find that the people who come to see me on days which are strongly under Saturn's influence usually have favors to ask or hard luck stories to tell. Saturn days are "beggars'" days—so much so that I have often threatened to see no one on those days but give myself over to study and research. But, of course, I *don't*—because I know that then more than ever is there need of astrology's constructive helpfulness.

For I have decided, after my many years of reading horoscopes and corresponding with people all over the globe, that the most useful thing astrology does for men and women is to help them when they are discouraged. If they know that some situation which is bothering them—either a general situation like the bad planetary conditions of the past few years or some individual affliction shown in their own horoscope—will clear up as soon as the stars change, they are bound to take courage, and fight on until more auspicious times.

There is a Fifth Avenue dressmaker, whose name is now known throughout the world of fashion, who came to me when he was under the worst kind of Saturnian conditions. He was absolutely discouraged; in fact, he was ready to close his shop and commit suicide. I remember working so hard to give him the courage to go on for a few weeks longer, assuring him that he had a great future in his business, if only he could last until he turned the corner from his bad aspects. He walked out of my studio a different man—and, of course, we all know what a success he has made. I sometimes think he could afford to keep me in gowns for the rest of my life,—but, alas, he doesn't!

Now, I have a special word for those of you who were born between December 23rd and January 20th—that is, in the sign Capricorn—because you are peculiarly under Saturn's disciplinary influence. Yours will be a life of overcoming obstacles and winning success through hard work; but if you cultivate your optimistic side and exercise the patience which your other planets give you, your progress will be steady and your success sure. The latter may come late in life. Saturn rules the aged. And it is a saying among astrologers that Saturn looks after his own!

If you were born between May 13th and 21st, or in the last ten days in July, or in the first ten days of October, you are also somewhat under Saturn, and must make every effort to counteract his depressing influence with patience and cheerfulness. If you do, you too will benefit from his practical, feet-on-the-ground, wisdom-giving qualities.

Earlier in this chapter, when I was talking about Saturn days, I counselled a waiting policy. This obviously does not apply to the entire lives of Saturn people. When aspects are temporary it is sometimes best to wait until they pass, but when they are permanent in the sense that they are a part of your destiny, you cannot afford to sit idly by and do nothing about it. And I certainly wouldn't advise you to do so.

I preach a gospel of action, not dependence.

I believe you should help the stars to help you. If you are under a favorable aspect of Mercury, for instance, you should place yourself under the very best conditions for mental accomplishment; if under Venus, you should go where you are likely to meet the type of people you wish to add to your rosary of friendship; if under Jupiter, you should go where fortunes are won. In other words, you should plant success if you wish to raise it.

If, on the other hand, you are under the more solemn influence of Saturn, and desire to court his higher vibrations, you should remember that his presence in your horoscope gives you unusual powers to accomplish things through hard work, that he enables you to materialize your mental and spiritual ideals on the material plane, that he is sure to be an increasingly favorable influence the further you go in your career, and that in all probability even his less attractive attributes are greatly modified in your individual chart by the influence of more cheerful and optimistic planets.

You should remember, too, that a great many men and women who have attained great fame have been born under the influence of this hard-working and practical planet. The late Marshal Joffre was such a man. So was Pasteur, Sir Isaac Newton, Admiral Dewey, King Edward VII, William E. Gladstone and Woodrow Wilson. So is Rudyard Kipling.

Mr. Gladstone, the great British Prime Minister, was a marked example of the Saturn nature at its best. He loved power, but his every act was tempered by mercy combined with justice. He considered himself a divine instrument, peculiarly adapted to solve the problems which beset the British Empire in his day. His tremendous self-control and gift for hard work enabled him to play the important part he did in the statesmanship of his time.

I could multiply these instances where the Saturn born have diverted their great gifts into the paths of accomplishment. But I think I have said enough at this point to prove that the stars do not condemn; they merely forewarn. It depends on how you act on the warnings that they give, whether you falter in your stride or press on, up the steep grade, to success. As I have said before, and will often say again: "You are not tied to the wheels of destiny. You are in this life to help the wheels go round!"

URANUS

"THE GOD OF INVENTION"

URANUS is the planet of science and invention. It rules over governments, associations and railroads. It is the reformer that destroys but to rebuild better anew. And finally, it is the erratic, nervous, unconventional planet, under whose influence we must never force matters, but rest content to take things as they come.

Its influence is quite different from thac of the phlegmatic and sometimes sinister Saturn. When Saturn is unfriendly, don't ask favors, don't start new enterprises, don't attend to anything of importance unless forced to do so. When Uranus is unfriendly don't get nervous and aggressive, don't put on pressure. Be *nonchalant!*

If you were born under the influence of this erratic planet, you are probably a duckling in a brood of chickens. Not an ugly duckling, you understand, because Uranus presides over Aquarius, one of the most beautiful of the signs of the Zodiac, but a duckling just the same. At least, you aren't any ordinary chicken!

Highly developed natures under the influence of Uranus aim at great and noble things, are fond of philosophical subjects, have strong intuitions, and desire to rise above the material. They are romantic, inventive, frequently prophetic. In short, they are extraordinary characters. On the other hand, the undeveloped Uranian is apt to be eccentric, brusque, reckless, headstrong, rebellious, out of tune with people and affairs. They are what we call "queer sticks."

179

It is important, therefore, for you to find out: first, whether or not you are a child of this erratic planet; and second, whether you are developed or undeveloped.

The first point I can answer—even without knowing your exact birthday—if you were born between January 21st and February 19th, because that is the period which is governed by the sign Aquarius; and Uranus is the ruling planet of that sign. The second point—unless I have more definite information as to the date of your birth—you will have to settle for yourself!

A great many other people besides the natives of Aquarius are also born with Uranus powerful in their horoscopes; and they, too, must be careful to court only its higher vibrations. If you find, on having your horoscope read by a competent astrologer, that you are such a person, you will probably succeed best in some occupation where the humanitarian impulse is an important factor. Many astrologers, research workers, scientific investigators, people who make a study of the undiscovered, are born strongly under this metaphysical planet.

Uranus stands for the higher octave; and in order to court its most favorable vibrations, it is essential to be without any ulterior motive. Like the sign Aquarius, over which it rules, it stands for Universal Brotherhood, and it is essential that those born strongly under it remain on the higher plane.

This planet which discards worn-out customs, breaks bonds and often brings about estrangements, was rising at the time our country was born. And that fact, as I have told elsewhere in this book, is an obvious explanation of why we, as a people, refused to continue under the dominion of England. Uranus also rules over electricity, the higher mathematics, and public institutions of all kinds.

Uranus completes a revolution of the twelve signs of the

Zodiac once in eighty-four years. As this planet stirs a spirit of revolution and rebellion, we naturally must look for a war for ideals or freedom once in every eighty-four years. It is only necessary to glance over the pages of history to find that Uranus was passing through the sign Gemini at the time of the American Revolution and again during the Civil War.

In the year 1942, Uranus once again enters the sign Gemini and unfortunately Saturn and Mars will also be in conjunction with it. It remains for the future to determine just what this combination of planetary force portends. In 1943 and 1944 Mars will also be in this sign. This unusual configuration certainly portends another period when this country will be plunged into war.

But Uranus is not always an upsetting influence, especially if it is combined favorably with other planets. And sometimes, of course, its effect is neither good nor bad, but merely indicates the unusual, the unexpected. For example, the most interesting thing to me, as an astrologer, in the horoscope of Andrée, the polar explorer whose body was discovered after many years, is that if he had lived, he would have been more strongly under the influence of Uranus at the time his body was found than at any time since the disaster. It was time, then, for the unexpected to happen to him—and it did. Even in death Andrée could not escape his stars.

NEPTUNE

"THE GOD OF VISION"

NEPTUNE is revolutionary, mystical, romantic, sometimes irresponsible, always remote. It causes nervousness and restlessness; lends itself often quite unconsciously to pretense and deceit; and inspires or disorganizes, according to the way we receive its powerful influences.

Neptune governs artistic, æsthetic and inspirational pursuits. It favors the pulpit, the rostrum, the stage or the screen. It governs diplomacy and aviation.

It is so vast, so slow, so mystical, so little understood that it is rightly called "The Shadow Planet."

Days when Neptune is in power are excellent for salesmen. At such time, insurance agents and promoters and all others depending on the silver tongue will be full of "pep." Look out for them, and make sure that any proposition you discuss with them is something you really want to do. If you don't, you may find that you have done the wrong thing before you know it. Their propositions may be honest enough, but not at all essential to your happiness. If, on the other hand, you are a salesman yourself, go to it. With Neptune's help, you could sell the Mayor of Roquefort a moon made out of green cheese!

Naturally, being the shadow planet—ruling camouflage, pretense—Neptune also rules the motion picture industry, whose business it is to present a counterfeit representation of life. Most picture stars were born strongly under the influence of Neptune. It was the latter's position in Rudolph Valentino's chart, for example, that made him a much more successful lover on the screen than in real life.

But the best example of Neptune's influence on a movie star is, perhaps, the late Lon Chaney. In Mr. Chaney's case, success of some sort in the theatre was fore-shadowed—you might say it was almost guaranteed—by the fact that his Jupiter (ruling money, glory, honor and success) was friendly to Venus (ruling entertainment and the arts). But the *type* of success which he achieved was indicated by the fact that his Mercury (ruling the intellect) was in Pisces (Neptune's sign) and in aspect to the Moon (ruling the public), to Uranus (ruling originality) and to Neptune itself (ruling camouflage, make-up, *and* the motion picture industry).

As is the case with most people born so strongly under Neptune, there was a natural secretiveness indicated in Lon Chaney's horoscope; and he was, as everybody knows, the motion picture star about whose private life and actual personality the public knew least. Even his best friends were never sure that they knew the real Lon Chaney. The uncanny power which he had to conceal his natural features behind the most bewildering variety of make-up known to modern theatricals seems to have extended to his personality. Like a true son of Neptune, he camouflaged himself so that even his best friends did not know him. And I should not be surprised if his wonderful knowledge of make-up died with him.

Incidentally, Mr. Chaney had Neptune in Taurus, ruling the throat, which gave him his extraordinary ability, revealed for the first time in his one and only talking picture, to place his voice after the manner of a ventriloquist. Most people who have succeeded in operatic and other purely vocal careers have been strongly under Taurus; and many of the world's greatest ventriloquists have had Neptune, as Lon Chaney had, in the throat sign.

Until 1928, Neptune had been for about fifteen years in

the sign Leo, which rules the theatre and all other forms of amusement. This position of the shadow planet accounts astrologically for the vast strides made by the shadow screen during those years. In 1928 Neptune passed over into Virgo, one of the factors which rules the voice; and it is significant that at just that time the talking pictures began engaging the thoughts and activities of the entire moving picture world. Since Neptune is due to remain in its present sign, Virgo, for another period of fifteen years, there will, no doubt, be marvelous improvements made in this field.

Another problem which must be met during Neptune's passage through Virgo is the question of labor and all matters pertaining to housing, feeding and clothing the public. The employer must do everything in his power to appeal to the intelligence and reason of those in his employ; and the laborer in every industry and profession must realize that if he is to hold his job, his demands must be within the bounds of reason. Both employee and employer must make money or the whole structure will fall and end in disaster for all concerned. It is not beyond the imagination to conceive that failure to heed these astrological warnings might be the cause of the war which is threatening within fifteen years.

The influence of Neptune in Virgo will also have a subtle and upsetting effect on the health. Neptune rules the cerebro-spinal nervous system, and Virgo rules the abdominal organs, including the diaphragm, bowels, spleen, and pancreas, and sympathetically the lungs, liver, hands, and feet. The individual should guard against going to extremes in overworking, and being too exacting or intolerant of the shortcomings or what appears to him to be the stupidity of others. Cerebro-spinal fever, spotted fever or meningitis may be prevalent during these fifteen years, as well as troubles which come as the result of poor elimination or the system becoming too depleted.

Psychiatrists, osteopaths, hydropathists, as well as those who employ mental therapy or drugless methods in curing diseases, may be more in demand than those who depend wholly on drugs as a method of cure. On the other hand the authorities may find it necessary to be more diligent than ever to suppress the traffic in drugs, as Neptune will not only stimulate the activity of the illicit drug dealers, but cause people who have any desire for narcotics to be willing to go to greater lengths in order to satisfy their abnormal craving.

Those who do research work and writers of fiction, particularly of a fanciful or semi-scientific and prophetic character—the Jules Verne and Marie Corelli types—will be stimulated by this position of Neptune. But if the imagination is not made use of constructively, either in literary work or otherwise, it may then have an upsetting effect on the nervous system. Where there is not a balance between the mental and physical, there will be danger of obsessions, false fears, and a tendency to exaggerate the importance of trifles.

Neptune always exerts its influence with special force on those born between February 20th and March 21st. But during its passage through Virgo, people born between the 20th and 24th of February, 21st and 25th of May, 23rd and 28th of August, 23rd and 27th of November of any year, will be especially responsive either favorably or the reverse to the vibrations of this planet.

Of course, Neptune's influence is not necessarily "bad." Nothing which gives vision, imagination, inspiration, could be wholly that. And sometimes, when combined with other planets, it endows its children with truly remarkable gifts. Don't forget, if you are a child of Neptune, that you are heir to the Kingdom of Vision!

THE HOUSES

*"On the East, three Gates;
on the North, three Gates;
on the South, three Gates;
and on the West, three Gates."*
—REVELATION, XXI, 13.

THE TWELVE HOUSES

AN EXPLANATION

EVERY effort has been made in this volume, which the publishers describe as a "popular" book on astrology, to avoid the technical phraseology with which the science of the stars has too long been enshrouded. Even the more common astrological terms like "trine" and "sextile" and "ascendant" have so far as possible been banished from these pages.

For this reason, and in order that this book should live up to its description, I have omitted all mention of the "Twelve Houses" which correspond in a general way to the "Twelve Signs." The signs are, as you know, divisions of time; the houses are divisions of space. But since the latter are quite as important as the former to the student of astrology, who wishes to go further in the science, I am appending a brief description which is taken from one of my other books, "Astrology: Your Place in the Sun," which, together with "Astrology: Your Place Among the Stars," treats the scientific side of the subject in much more detail.

Description of The Twelve Houses.

Ascendant.—The first house, which mundanely is Aries, and ruled over by Mars, signifies man's outward appearance and everything which has to do with the personality. It rules the head and determines the degree of activity or repression of the individual. In questions pertaining to the affairs of nations, and universal conditions generally, the first house signifies the masses, or general state of that locality or kingdom where the figure is erected.

189

The House of Money.—The second house, which mundanely is Taurus and ruled over by Venus, signifies the financial circumstances or fortune, profit or gain, loss or damage, and all movable goods of the individual. It rules the throat and determines the degree of prosperity which the native will enjoy. In questions pertaining to the affairs of nations or conditions generally, the second house signifies national wealth, banking activities and matters which concern revenue in general.

House of Relatives.—The third house, which mundanely is Gemini and ruled over by Mercury, signifies brothers, sisters, neighbours, environment of the family, short journeys, correspondence and messages of all kinds, the degree of mentality, perception and adaptability of the individual, and determines the native's relations with all these departments. It rules the shoulders, arms, hands and fingers. In questions pertaining to national affairs, it rules over transportation, whether it be by railways, common carriers, post office, telegraph, telephone or radio. It also stands for libraries and public education generally.

The House of the Home.—The fourth house, which mundanely is Cancer, and ruled over by the Moon, signifies the father or mother, inherited tendencies, the environment during the early childhood and old age, fixed possessions, such as real estate, of the individual. It rules the stomach and breast, and determines the native's relations with his father and mother, environment, and the state of his property holdings. In questions pertaining to national affairs, it rules over mines, agriculture, gardens, crops, public buildings, and determines the termination or end of anything.

The House of Pleasure.—The fifth house, which mundanely is Leo, and ruled over by the Sun, signifies love affairs, entertainment, speculation, and children, of the individual. It rules the heart and back, and determines the degree of success or failure in the native's love affairs and pleasures, his speculative operations, and matters concerning offspring. In questions pertaining to national affairs, it rules over ambassadors, banquets, theaters, and education generally.

The House of Health and Service.—The sixth house, which mundanely is Virgo, and ruled over by Mercury, signifies the needs, afflictions, and care of the body, servants, inferiors, dress and hygiene, grandparents, uncles and aunts, and domestic animals, of the individual. It rules the intestines and solar plexus, and determines the state of the native's health, his ability to get on with servants and inferiors, and his relations with grandparents, uncles and aunts, and small animals. In questions pertaining to national affairs, it rules over the working classes generally; over industries, public health and sanitation.

The House of Marriage and Partnerships.—The seventh house, which mundanely is Libra, and ruled over by Venus, signifies marriage, business partnerships, and public enemies, of the individual. It rules the veins, the kidneys (and in the case of a woman, the ovaries), and determines the degree of happiness and success derived through marriage and partnerships, and the type of public enemies the native may have. In questions pertaining to national affairs, it rules over foreign relations, peace, war and international relationships.

The House of Death.—The eighth house, which mundanely is Scorpio, and ruled over by Mars, signifies the inheritance, legacies, wills and the goods of the dead, of the individual. It rules the organs of generation, and determines all questions regarding inheritance, and the type of death of the native. In questions pertaining to national affairs, it signifies the death of national rulers, and matters that may be involved because of such deaths.

The House of Religion and Philosophy.—The ninth house, which mundanely is Sagittarius, and ruled over by Jupiter, signifies religion, philosophy, long journeys, particularly by water, and the relations with foreigners, of the individual. It has rule over abstract thought, dreams and visions, as distinguished from the concrete concerns of the third house. It rules the hips and thighs, and determines the religion and philosophical beliefs of the native, and the amount of travel and success he will enjoy in distant countries. In questions pertaining to national affairs, it rules over churches, law-courts, shipping, cables, and the findings of science.

The House of Business and Honor.—The tenth house, which mundanely is Capricorn, and ruled over by Saturn, signifies ambition, fame, worldly position, power, promotion, elevation, the calling or authority, of the individual. It also signifies either the father or mother, as in the fourth house. (Some authorities claim that the fourth house rules the father, and the tenth the mother, but the author has not been able to prove that this is correct.) It rules the skeleton, and particularly the knees, and determines the degree of success in business and the honor of the native. In questions pertaining to national affairs, it rules over the upper classes, or those in power and authority (as did the sixth house the masses and those who serve), rulers, such as presidents, kings and dictators.

The House of Friends.—The eleventh house, which mundanely is Aquarius and ruled over by Uranus, signifies the friendships and the aspirations of the individual. It rules the legs, particularly the ankles, and determines the native's relations with friends, his position toward humanity, and the degree of harmony or inharmony of life in relation to his fellowman. In questions pertaining to national affairs it rules over the counselors, associates or allies of the nation.

The House of Secret Enemies.—The twelfth house, which

mundanely is Pisces, and ruled over by Neptune, signifies unseen difficulties, impairment of the senses, seclusion, forced or otherwise, and secret enemies of the individual. It rules the extremities, and determines the amount of freedom enjoyed by the native, and the degree to which he will be forced to submerge his own personality, in his subservience to others. In questions pertaining to national affairs, it rules prisons, hospitals and asylums, and all matters pertaining to such institutions.

"It is only by the vision of wisdom that the horoscope of the ages can be read."
—EMERSON.

END OF PART I

PART TWO

ASTROLOGY—HOW IT WORKS

"Whosoever may be adapted to any particular event or pursuit will assuredly have the star indicative thereof very potent in his nativity."
—PTOLEMY.

"It is the stars, the stars above us, Govern our conditions."
—SHAKESPEARE.

"Hitch your wagon to a star."
—EMERSON.

OTHER PEOPLE'S STARS

SOME FAMOUS WOMEN

In the preceding chapters we have been discussing chiefly your own stars and how to know them. But at this point, I should like to switch for a while to other people's stars—first of all, to certain famous people's, whose lives are the best possible evidence of the way the horoscope determines our careers.

For example, I noticed not so long ago that Jane Addams, the Chicago philanthropist who is considered by many the greatest woman of her generation, was having a birthday. It was years since I had consulted Miss Addams' horoscope, and it was with something like a thrill that I recalled that her Jupiter was in Leo—a condition which always brings about generous impulses, and doubtless accounts in her case for her willingness to devote herself to the welfare of others; that her Moon was in Taurus friendly, as we astrologers say, to Mars and also to Neptune, which accounts for her interest in the masses and her great executive ability; that her Sun is unfriendly to Uranus, which may account for her never having married, and certainly indicates that she is very fortunate in not having done so; and that her Venus was in Cancer in aspect to Mars, which may well account for her being so interested in the welfare of children. I will not take your time to give the technical explanation of why this is so, but if there are any astrologers reading these words, they will see at once that Miss Jane Addams is a striking witness to the truths that have come down to us from the Chaldeans and the Babylonians.

The same thing is true of another Miss Adams—this time, spelled in the traditional Boston manner—our well-beloved Maude Adams, whose Moon is in the ambitious sign Aries and friendly to the inspirational Uranus and the intellectual Mercury. Her Mercury is in the discriminating sign Sagittarius and is also friendly to Uranus, causing her to live much within herself and to derive her most congenial companionship from the creatures of her imagination. She cares little for contacts with people, and it is not strange that she has chosen to live what should have been the years of her greatest artistic fulfillment "far from the madding crowd." Her Venus is in Sagittarius, too, sometimes called the bachelor sign, but it is friendly to Neptune, the planet which enables people to act what they really do not feel. It was the Neptune influence which made her so convincing as Maggie in "What Every Woman Knows"; and it was Neptune, combined with Uranus, which gave us her "Peter Pan."

You can imagine, can't you, what a thrill this sort of thing gives to an astrologer? It is, so to speak, life's final check on the truth of the science, the best of all proofs of how astrology works. It is in that last capacity that I am going to analyze briefly the horoscopes of several other famous men and women in this and the following chapter. There is no better way to show how the signs and the planets work—on each other and on mankind.

Katharine Cornell is an even better example than Maude Adams of the astrological secrets which the individual horoscopes disclose. Miss Cornell was born with the Moon in Aquarius—which isn't in itself especially favorable to acting. Sir Henry Irving and Jack Barrymore are the only other Aquarian persons, whose stage successes occur to me as I write. But Miss Cornell has an individual horoscope which shows that she would be successful in anything she undertook to do. She was born on the new Moon, one of the

most favorable times in the whole month. And such a
Moon! Jupiter, the Greater Fortune, is smiling on it. And
Jupiter confers honor, success, plenty, supremacy. Moreover, the Sun, which rules her relations with men, is favorable to her Jupiter, indicating that the men with whom she
is associated, especially the man to whom she is married,
will be most influential in her success. Another favorable
planet in Miss Cornell's horoscope is Mercury, ruling the
intellect. That is why she turns every now and then from
her sure-fire Jupiter successes like "The Green Hat" and
"Dishonored Lady" to such intellectual plays as "The Bar-
retts of Wimpole Street" and Shaw's "Candida." Like you
and me, and all the rest of the world, she cannot deny her
stars.

To turn for a moment from the women of the stage, let
us consider Mrs. Carrie Chapman Catt, heroine of that
"Votes for Women" campaign which now seems so far back
in the distant past, and still head and front of all movements for the advancement of the feminine side of the
human race. She was born on January 9th, when the Moon
was in Pisces in conjunction with Neptune and Mars. No
wonder she had the vision to foresee the emancipation of
women and the courage to fight for it! No wonder, too,
with her favorable aspect of Mars, that she has now turned
her energies into the fight against war! There are other
aspects in Mrs. Catt's chart which fortify and strengthen
those which I have just mentioned. She has Mercury, the
planet ruling the mind, in the forward-looking sign Sagittarius, and friendly to Neptune, the God of Vision. Mrs.
Catt has always been in advance of her times. Her public
life is the best known example of this trait, but I venture
to say that her domestic affairs are ordered in the same
manner. If her house isn't equipped with every modern,
labor-saving and comfort-giving device, she is not as true to

her stars as I believe her to be. She also has Venus in Sagittarius, a most impersonal sign, which frees her from many personal temptations and leaves her free to lavish her nature on the world. It is interesting to note that at just the time when she was presented with a five thousand dollar check as the "woman of the year," her Jupiter, the planet which rules honor, glory, success and wealth, was friendly to both her Moon and her Neptune, a most advantageous position in her chart.

I emphasize the Moon in the charts of these public women because the Moon rules both the public *and* woman. It is not always the dominating influence, however.

Queen Victoria had the Moon in Gemini, but, generally speaking, her planets were much more evenly distributed among the signs. Her Mercury, ruling the mind, was in Taurus, indicating her stubborn determination to have her own way. She had Saturn in Pisces which made her physically "squatty," and Jupiter in Aquarius, which gave her humanitarian instincts. One of the most revealing things in this horoscope is the position of Venus. We don't usually associate Queen Victoria with Venus, but she had one, and it was in the sign Aries, which made her a stickler for the conventions—which, a whole generation can testify, she certainly was. But her Venus was also in favorable aspect to Uranus, the erratic planet, under whose influence anything may happen. Hence, Victoria's much discussed intimate friendship with the Scotch gilly, John Brown. Even a queen must reckon with the stars—especially with her Venus.

Isadora Duncan, on the other hand, although born when the Sun was in Gemini, has her Moon—as you might expect —in the idealistic, pioneer sign Aries, indicating the imaginative and daring quality of her life and work. And that is not all; Venus, the planet which played so large a part in Miss Duncan's life, was in aspect to the erratic Uranus when she was born, suggesting the extreme unconventionality, even eccentricity, which marked her personal life.

Mary Pickford has her Sun in the same sign where Miss Duncan had her Moon—Aries, the sign of leadership. Aries people get to the top. Aries people lend themselves to publicity. That is why more famous movie actors and actresses were born under Aries than under any other sign. The Aries-born just naturally seek the limelight, or if they don't seek it, they are thrust into it. The same thing is true outside of the movies. Chief Justice Hughes is a good example. So is Secretary Mellon. So is Nicholas Murray Butler. So *was* J. P. Morgan, the elder.

Mary is especially well equipped to take advantage of her Aries opportunities because she has Jupiter, the planet which rules money, glory and success, in that sign, in conjunction with the strength-giving Sun and in aspect to the aggressive, determined Mars. Mary's Venus, which is in the mental sign Gemini, is also in conjunction with Neptune, the planet which rules the motion picture industry and the whole art of make-believe. Her Moon, which rules her relations with the public, is in the vigorous sign Taurus, which rules the throat and therefore the talking pictures. With Jupiter and the Sun in conjunction in Aries, Miss Pickford could hardly fail to win success in some public endeavor. With Venus, the planet which rules entertainment, in conjunction with Neptune, she could hardly fail to win success on the shadow stage. With the Moon, ruling the public, in the sign which rules the throat, she could hardly fail to win success in the talkies, or on the so-called legitimate stage.

In the case of Dowager Queen Marie of Roumania, it is her Mercury, ruling the mind, which presents the most interesting aspect to an astrologer. It is in the deep and sometimes devious sign Scorpio, indicating that she not only has abundant ability to take care of herself in the sphere in which she is called upon to move, but is possessed by the desire to shine in literary circles. As a matter of fact, she has, like her predecessor, Carmen Sylva, already obtained a considerable reputation as a writer—usually as a collaborator. Not a few American journalists have returned to America with volumes written "in collaboration with the Queen of Roumania." In Bucharest it is explained that the Queen has a system: The visitor writes his book or play, leaving a gap, a short chapter or a scene, outlined but not absolutely written; and the Queen looks over the rough notes, and dictates from them to a stenographer. Under this system her participation in the work may be only a few lines or pages, but the publication of the manuscript is good press-agency work. It gets Roumania known and doesn't hurt the Queen.

These indications which show up so clearly in an individual's horoscope are sometimes amazing to the uninitiated. I remember a skeptical caller once gave me the date of an unknown man. I said: "This is a student and a scholar. Whatever success he has attained, he has won by his brains." My caller laughed in triumph; and gave me another date, this time that of a woman. "Here," I said, "is a born actress. She couldn't help acting whether she was on the stage or not." The caller looked chagrined. The man was E. H. Sothern—and my client thought I had failed on him because I had said he was a student and a scholar, whereas, as any dramatic critic will tell you, Mr. Sothern is *just* that, and gets all his effects on the stage by his intellectual hold on his audiences. His wife, on the other hand—for the second date proved to be that of Miss Julia Marlowe—has the divine fire of true histrionic greatness—the fire that Duse had and Bernhardt in her prime—and it shows in her eyes, in her voice, in her lovely hands, and in her horoscope. I tell this story not for my own glory—any competent astrologer could have read those two charts as I read them—but merely to indicate how impossible it is to get away from your stars.

It used to be a favorite sport, before astrology recovered its lost prestige as a science, to "go up to Carnegie Hall and try to fool Evangeline Adams" as this woman who gave me the Sothern and Marlowe dates undoubtedly tried to do. I have told elsewhere about the woman who gave me the names of two children, and how I said just as soon as I looked at their charts: "It's no use drawing these horoscopes. The persons are dead." Then I added: "Probably by drowning." They turned out to be Isadora Duncan's two children who had met their death by plunging from an automobile into the River Arno! And I recall, as I write, Laurette Taylor bringing me a birthdate once and *not* telling me that it belonged to "Michael," the famous dog which appeared with her in "Peg o' My Heart." But you can't fool astrology on the things that count! I told Miss Taylor that the person she was inquiring about would have an extraordinary life, that he or she was probably born in a hut, and would live in a palace, that he would profit largely through some woman close to his life, that he would have no interest in books but would learn best from travel and experience, that he had decided dramatic ability and might play important parts on the stage, and that he would live to be a ripe old age. Well, you know "Michael"! If you saw the play or the picture, you could never forget him! He was born in a cheap tenement on New York's East Side, and he spent his later life in what was for a dog, palatial luxury. He certainly profited through a woman. He presumably had no interest in books. He has traveled all over this country and Europe, and has had the most extraordinary experiences; been on the stage, played in pictures in Hollywood, spent four months in Quarantine, and so on and so on. No one could doubt his dramatic ability—and as for longevity, when I last heard from him and his famous mistress, he had achieved the noble canine age of seventeen.

But to get back to our famous women: Miss Ruth Draper's Moon, unlike Mr. Sothern's is very friendly to Neptune, giving her her unusual ability for original work on the stage. You are aware, of course, of her unprecedented ability to hold an audience for a whole evening, with almost no help from settings or costumes, by her own unaided art of character projection. Her Moon is not in such a brilliant sign as Mr. Sothern's but it is in one which contributes to her ability to do any kind of hard work. Her Mercury, ruling the mind, is in a sign which accounts for her lighter side and her ability to bring comedy into her work and mirth into her audiences. She should be remarkably free from temptations which might divert her from her work. Her Jupiter, which rules over wealth and success, is in the lordly sign Leo and friendly to the Sun. She can hardly fail to make money through her efforts. But she is not stingy. I should not be surprised if she was exceedingly generous to the members of her own family.

It is interesting to note that Mrs. Fiske has the Moon in the same sign that Miss Draper has it, and she also has Mercury and Jupiter in that sign, the hard-working and self-deprecating Capricorn. Mrs. Fiske's long history on the stage, her proficiency in many difficult parts, her indefatigable pursuit of dramatic perfection are of course sufficient evidence that she is the hard-working person her horoscope says she is. And as for her modesty, everybody who knows her will tell you that it amounts to a passion. I remember going with her as her guest to a theatrical box party, and later to a reception in the St. Regis Hotel. At both places, she insisted on hiding herself in an inconspicuous corner and doing everything she could to conceal the fact that so distinguished a person was the Hamlet of the party. The fact that she has so many planets in Capricorn, which is ruled by the solemn planet Saturn, and in conjunction with Jupiter the God of Success and friendly to Neptune which rules the stage, accounts not only for her great versatility and continued success in the theatre, but also for the fact that she has taken her art so seriously, even though she doesn't take *herself* seriously at all. A most engaging horoscope— and not the least interesting fact about it is that she has two important planets in the sign ruling animals. I mention this fact because of Mrs. Fiske's life-long interest in behalf of our dumb friends. You will recall that it was she who led the storm of protest which went up all over the country at an ill-considered proposal to establish bull-fighting on American soil.

This chapter has rather run to ladies of the stage. The reason, of course, is that they are more willing than some others to be discussed in the public prints. But I assure you that the same deadly parallels between the horoscope and life occur in the charts of people in every walk of life. As evidence that this is so, I ask you to compare the horoscopes of Eva Le Gallienne, the actress-manager, and Professor William James, the great philosopher of blessed memory. At first glance, they would seem to have little in common except that they were born on the same day of the month, the eleventh of January, but it happens that they are a good deal alike. They both have the Moon in Capricorn, the hard-working sign, and certainly both the actress and the professor have been among the workers of the world. This Capricorn influence indicates that both would take their work seriously; and this, too, has invariably been true. Professor James, who had a delightful sense of humor and a lightness of touch which would have made him fully as successful in the field of fiction as was his brother, Henry James, turned instead to the deepest kind of philosophical writing. Miss Le Gallienne, fresh from Broadway successes in delightful trifles like "The Swan," chose to bury herself in the work of her Civic Repertory Theatre on Fourteenth Street, where she has made a hard-won success by producing serious dramas and tragedies, which the Broadway managers would not touch.

This unusual pair are as remarkable in their divergencies as they are in their likenesses. Professor James not only had the Moon in Capricorn, as Miss Le Gallienne has, but he also had Mercury, Venus, Jupiter and Saturn. Having so many planets in such a sign of service and hard work undoubtedly limited the professor's life very materially so far as social matters went, and intensified the serious side of his character. Miss Le Gallienne, on the other hand, has the Moon in conjunction with the Sun in the house of money; she has Venus in Sagittarius in conjunction with Uranus, the planet which rules dramatics; and she has Mercury also in Sagittarius in aspect to Neptune, the planet which rules the stage. Was anybody's career ever more clearly indicated by anything than this girl's by her stars? And is it any wonder that while the professor was struggling in his solemn way to find out the secret of life, the actress was storming the heights of play-acting and unreality? Another thing which Miss Le Gallienne has is a most favorable Jupiter. It is this planet which has enabled her to secure endowments for her theatre, and to keep on its feet an enterprise which Broadway wiseacres long since doomed to the oblivion of Mr. Cain's theatrical store-house.

In the year 1930, on Miss Le Gallienne's birthday, I had occasion to say something publicly in regard to her horoscope; and after telling what a splendid example she was of how we all fulfill our stars, I added: "She is coming under aspects during 1931 which should warn her against working too hard. She mustn't let her ambition push her during 1931 at the expense of her health, for if she saves herself for the following year, 1932, Jupiter will be waiting for her with some of the biggest opportunities of her career." Several months later, when even I had forgotten my reading of her stars, someone called my attention to a clipping from a New York newspaper, which carried this headline: "Eva Le Gallienne to Take Year's Rest.   After Five Years of Directing Civic Repertory Theatre, Her Health Requires Vacation."

What I didn't say about Miss Le Gallienne's indications for this particular period—because I never do say such things in public utterances about living people—was that she was coming under conditions most unfavorable to her health and general welfare and that she should protect herself against dangers and injuries, not only from overwork, but from every cause whatsoever.   I was not surprised, therefore, to read another piece about Miss Le Gallienne in the same paper several months later, telling of a serious accident in which she had received serious burns from which she recovered only after long and painful weeks in the hospital.   Now that it is all over, I can offer this incident as one more evidence of how minutely the horoscope foretells life!

OTHER PEOPLE'S STARS

SOME FAMOUS MEN

CALVIN COOLIDGE was born on the Fourth of July. A quiet man on a noisy day! But on the particular Fourth of July that Mr. Coolidge was born, July 4, 1872, the stars were quiet, if the fire-crackers weren't. In fact, four of his most important planets were in Cancer, the most silent of all the signs in the Zodiac. He is, therefore, for this and other reasons, an excellent example of the way the stars influence man.

Cancer people are conservative, home-loving, domestic, tenacious, prudent, reflective, serene *and* silent. They are also personally ambitious, and inclined to public life. Jupiter, which as you know, governs success, honors and position in life, was in the lordly sign Leo, the royal sign, when Mr. Coolidge was born, so there was every good reason to believe that he would achieve the very highest rank in whatever line he undertook. His Jupiter was also friendly to Uranus, the God of Luck, which accounts for what we have come to know as *"Coolidge Luck."* His Moon, ruling women, was in Gemini, ruling diplomacy, and in conjunction with Mars, ruling energy, courage, determination, strength. This combination accounts for his clever, diplomatic wife, and the great part she has played in his successful career. Mrs. Coolidge's own horoscope completes the picture, because her Moon was in Taurus, friendly to Venus, which gave her her beauty and charm.

Those of you who are familiar with the workings of astrology will not be surprised that Mr. Coolidge's horoscope, like those of the famous women we discussed in the preceding chapter, gives such an accurate picture of his character and career. But even you may be surprised that the three things about Mr. Coolidge which have been most often mentioned—his wife, his luck and his silence—were so very clearly indicated in the astrological heavens on the day he was born. Even I, an old hand at astrology, have to smile a bit when I think that he had four planets in silent Cancer. No wonder they say he used to weigh his words and now he counts them!

Mr. Coolidge's friend, Senator Borah, was another born with three planets in Cancer; but he was also strongly under Taurus, the sign which rules the throat. You can draw your own conclusions from this fact! Even the Cancer planets have a different effect on him than they do on Mr. Coolidge, because they are all in friendly aspect to the revolutionary planet, Neptune. Neptune makes him a leader of the progressives; but the fact that so many important planets are in the conservative Cancer causes him to line up every once in a while with the conservatives. The inherent conservatism in his nature also comes out in his personal life. The Senator neither smokes nor drinks. He doesn't even drink coffee. Like all people born strongly under Taurus, he is loyal so long as the other fellow does not—in his opinion—betray his confidence or fail to live up to his promises. But once he turns, he turns. The Senator's Moon is in Virgo, an earth sign, which accounts for his interest in the farmer. It is also friendly to Venus, which accounts for the important part which *his* charming and popular wife has played in his career.

Elihu Root, a statesman of a slightly earlier period but still a great figure as these words are written, had five important planets—Mercury, Venus, Neptune, Saturn and the Sun—all in the sign Aquarius at the time he was born.

This grouping of the planets in one sign is a very common thing in the horoscopes of men fated to play a major rôle in the conduct of the world's affairs; and when the grouping is in such a sign as Aquarius, a career of unselfish, unseeking public service such as Mr. Root's is clearly foreshadowed at the moment of birth. It is unnecessary to go into the various interrelations between these planets to realize how Elihu Root has fulfilled this promise of his stars. It *is* interesting to note, however, that he was destined by the position of the planets when he was born—particularly by the close conjunction of the Sun and Neptune—not only to enjoy his great gifts while he was young but to preserve them to a grand old age.

Another grand old man, President von Hindenburg, is a prime example of how the horoscope works out in human life. He was born with the Moon in Cancer, the same sign in which Hugo Stinnes, his great compatriot, had it. Theodore Roosevelt had the Moon in this sign; but most of those who are born with the Moon so placed are of the slower-moving, ponderous type, like Von Hindenburg, whose minds, though never idle, are inclined to be meditative. It is a very strong position for the Moon, because Cancer is her own sign, and she is stronger in it than in any other. The fact that she is also friendly to Jupiter in Von Hindenburg's horoscope is, therefore, one of the controlling factors in his destiny.

The Moon rules the masses, and Jupiter rules success. The old general's appeal to the masses is explained by the friendliness of these two planets. Among so-called experts Ludendorff was considered a more important leader than Hindenburg; but to the world at large, Hindenburg was the hero of the German side of the war. It was *his* statue that they raised in honor and glory; and it was *his* name that they cheered on every occasion; and when the time came, it was *his* person that they installed in the great stone house on the Williamstrasse.

One of Marshal von Hindenburg's chief opponents in the Great War, our own General Pershing, has Mercury, the planet which rules the mind, in Virgo unfriendly to Uranus, a combination which makes him highly critical and endlessly analytical. It is impossible for a man with a Mercury like that to be satisfied with anything but the most exhaustive treatment of any subject which interests him—and, as everyone in the literary world knows, General Pershing's memoirs were in preparation for the better part of ten years! The same planetary influence sometimes makes a person critical and sarcastic in his relations with other people and robs him of some of the popularity which his actual achievements deserve. But there is another side to the General's nature, about which the public knew little at the time of the War, but which became more evident in later years when so many of his associates and friends, who bore with him the burden of these days in France, were called to their graves; at such times, General Pershing showed a tenderness, a strong feeling of sentiment, a generous willingness to give credit where credit is due, a real capacity for affection. And this softer side of the Commander of the A.E.F. is undoubtedly due to the fact that Venus, goddess of the affections, was in the noble sign Leo when he was born.

To switch abruptly from military warfare to journalistic, let us consider the case of Arthur Brisbane, who has the Moon in Gemini in opposition to the Sun. That is where Joan of Arc had it; and many another crusader, who has influenced the history or the thought of the world. His Mercury, ruling his mind and also his writing, is in the practical, industrious sign Capricorn, but friendly to Neptune, the God of originality and vision. This is an ideal endowment for a writer who must combine, as Mr. Brisbane does, originality of thought and expression with the daily grind of newspaper production. His Jupiter is in Sagittarius rather close to the Sun, indicating that he can turn his abilities into financial gain and inasmuch as he is said to be the highest salaried newspaper writer in the world's history, there would seem to be little room for doubt as to the truth of that indication. Mr. Brisbane's Sun is in opposition to Uranus and friendly to Saturn, a condition which usually means that a man gets on well with both conservatives and radicals.

Another man who had Mercury in Capricorn was Lord Byron; but he had so many conflicting influences in his chart that it is no wonder Macaulay said of him: "He had a head which statuaries loved to copy, and a foot the deformity of which the beggars in the streets mimicked." And his mind was just as various as his physical conformation. "From the poetry of Lord Byron," wrote a great English commentator, "they drew a system of ethics compounded of misanthropy and voluptuousness—a system in which the two great commandments were to hate your neighbor and to love your neighbor's wife."

You may have some idea from these brief descriptions of the kind of man Lord Byron was. Now, look at his chart! He had the Moon in Cancer afflicted by Mars, Uranus and Mercury. That was enough to make him a genius. It was, in fact, more than enough, because it made him a thoroughly unbalanced person. Then, Mercury, which rules the mind, was in Capricorn, also afflicted by Uranus and Mars. It was as if the heavenly bodies, having decided to wreck this man's career, had made assurance doubly sure by dooming him to live in an imaginary world of his own, always seeking some new pleasure of the senses and—because of other and wholly contradictory influences in his horoscope. always meeting with defeat.

Those contradictory influences, which made him in his work rise above the standards established by his own life and enabled him to write such beautiful things as "Maid of Athens, ere we part, give, oh, give me back my heart!" had to do with the sign Aquarius. His Sun was in this humanitarian sign; and, of course, this gave him the finer side of his character which found expression in his works instead of in his deeds. His Venus was also in Aquarius in conjunction with Saturn, one of the very best combinations for a poet. With all this Aquarian influence, in spite of the bad aspects to the contrary, he couldn't help being a poet and a beautiful one at that!

You see, Walt Whitman was right; a truly great person is often all four sides to the square. But the lesson for us ordinary mortals to draw from such a horoscope as this would seem to be that we all have in some degree differing and contradictory aspects in our charts. The great thing is to know what these are so that we may encourage the good and discourage the bad. Especially the latter, for, as philosophers have always held, a recognized fault is a fault half overcome.

An excellent example of contrasting and apparently conflicting influences in a horoscope is to be found in the chart of Jascha Heifetz, the violinist. Everyone who has seen Heifetz, as well as heard him, has undoubtedly been impressed with his "poker face." Some may have thought that it indicated coldness or indifference or lack of emotional depth. Not at all. It indicates that Scorpio was rising at his birth; that it is his nature to wear a mask; that he would rather die than reveal his real feelings to the world. So, while violinists like Kreisler mirror in their faces the ecstasy which they experience in their souls, the great Heifetz must conceal his emotions behind a cold and apparently unseeing eye. But the sign which was rising at the time of your birth decides *only* your personality, your superficial appearance to the world; it has nothing to do with your individuality, with your character, with the real *you*. And so it is with Heifetz. Superficially, he is as his audiences see him; secretive, unresponsive Scorpio, the sign which represents water in its frozen sta.e. Actually, he is Aquarius, the sign of the man who pours himself out, as Heifetz does in his violin playing, on the whole world. Those who know Jascha Heifetz best know how true he is in his artistic and personal life to this Aquarian influence.

There are two other elements in Mr. Heifetz's horoscope, which have been so influential in moulding his *past* that they stand out, to an astrologer at least, as the most interesting of all. Mars, the most powerful of Mr. Heifetz's planets, was at the moment of his birth in that portion of the heavens ruling foreigners and foreign land—and we all know that he had to journey all the way from his native Russia to win the recognition that his great talents so richly deserved. That is one of the two elements to which I refer. The other, and even more important one, is that his Moon (ruling the public) was in its strongest sign, Cancer, and friendly to Uranus, the planet which rules public figures. I am not underestimating the part which Mr. Heifetz's extraordinary gifts as a super-violinist have played in his success, when I say that the *immediate recognition* which they received, when he first appeared in this country as a boy violinist, was undoubtedly due to this unusual combination of planetary conditions governing his relations with the public to which he was making his appeal.

Another interesting case in the artistic world was that of Oscar Wilde. On October 16, 1854, when Mr. Wilde was born, the Moon was afflicted by Uranus, which means that anything might happen. And in Mr. Wilde's life, almost everything did. Moreover, his Venus was in the detached,

impersonal, experimental sign Libra.   In these two aspects
lie the explanation, according to the stars, of Oscar Wilde's
eccentric personality, his strange life, his friendship with
Lord Alfred Douglas, his lawsuit against the Marquis of
Queensberry, his celebrated stay in Reading jail, his whole
disappointing career of shame and disgrace.   But there were
other aspects in Oscar Wilde's chart which as clearly indicate
all that was *glorious* in his literary and social career.   His
Mercury (ruling the mind) was in Scorpio, a shrewd, penetrating, critical and discriminating sign, and in aspect to the
mystical Neptune and the occult Uranus.   A person born
with Mercury so placed could not help being, as Wilde was, a
brilliantly clever man with a vision into the inner meaning
of life.   His Sun, governing the individuality, was also in
Libra, the sign of beauty, and absolutely unafflicted—hence,
his grace of manner and unforgettable charm.   "I have
known more heroic souls," writes his latest biographer, "and
some deeper souls—souls much more keenly alive to ideas of
duty and generosity; but I have known no more charming,
no more quickening, no more delightful spirit."   Poor Oscar
Wilde, his faults and his virtues were written in his stars!

Eugene O'Neill, author of "A Strange Interlude," was
born on the same day of the month as Oscar Wilde—but
in a different year, of course—and he presents an even more
interesting astrological study to us moderns.   He, too, has
Mercury in Scorpio, giving him the same penetrating mentality as Wilde's; but in Mr. O'Neill's case, there is an aspect
of Saturn which makes him more scientific and concrete
and less emotional in his method of expression.   It is too
bad, in a sense, that Mr. O'Neill's brilliant mind is not subject to vibrations of either Neptune or Uranus, for then he
would be able to give still loftier expression to his marvelous
conceptions.   Don't misunderstand me.   Eugene O'Neill,
the man, is essentially spiritual.   His Sun (ruling the in-

dividuality) is in conjunction with Uranus, the planet of genius. But one always feels, after seeing one of his wonderful plays, that he has stopped just short of giving visual expression to the spiritual loftiness that is written in every line of his soulful countenance. Mr. O'Neill's Moon (ruling the public) is friendly to Venus (ruling entertainment), and so is his Mercury (ruling the mind); so it was inevitable that he should use his great mental gifts to entertain the theatregoing public.

George Bernard Shaw's Venus is in Leo, together with his Sun, a planetary combination which tends to make anyone who has it very young for his age and also gives a merry, humorous side to the personality. His Mercury, which rules his mind, is friendly to Neptune, the God of originality; and Jupiter, the greater fortune, is in Aries, the sign which rules the British Isles—which indicates that Mr. Shaw, who has never hesitated to say what he thinks about his fellow countrymen, has probably been a greater benefit to the English people than they realize. Mr. Shaw's Saturn is in Cancer, indicating that his stomach is his weakest point and that he should study the question of diet as well as philosophy!

Mr. Shaw's fellow countryman—if an Irishman is willing to accept an Englishman in that guise!—his Royal Highness, the Prince of Wales, was born with the Moon in Pisces, which gives him what is, for a Prince, the priceless gift of popularity with the masses. Authors who attain a wide reading public often have this figure in their charts. In the Prince's horoscope, however, the Moon is also favorable to his Sun, which gives him success with nobles and dignitaries, suggests the high position which he is destined to occupy, and indicates an important career having to do with large matters. The Moon is also friendly to Uranus, which may account for the unusual life that he has led. It *is* unusual, you know, for an heir to a throne to reach his forties and still be unmarried. The Prince's Venus is in Taurus, which accounts for his popularity with the opposite sex; but the Uranian influence makes him interested in older or married women or those who, for one reason or another, are not in line to share his throne. A semi-humorous aspect in his chart is that his Sun is unfriendly to Mars which means that he is susceptible to accidents—such, for instance, as falling off his horse.

It is customary, when mentioning the Prince of Wales, to discuss also our own great young man, Colonel Lindbergh; but the Colonel so dislikes having himself and his affairs discussed that I have decided to turn instead to Admiral Byrd as an example of how the horoscope of the true adventurer cannot be denied. Our youngest and handsomest Admiral has both Venus and Jupiter, the lesser and the greater fortune, in the idealistic sign Sagittarius and in favorable aspect to the adventurous Neptune, sometimes called the God of Aviation. He has Uranus, the God of exploration, in that portion of the heavens ruling foreign lands, especially southern lands; and the same thing is true of his Sun and Mercury. This condition indicates success through travel in all parts of the world, but particularly in those portions of the globe south of his place of birth. Byrd succeeded in his flights to Europe and across the North Pole because of his generally favorable aspects for such undertakings. But he couldn't help succeed in his search for the South Pole, because success by southern travel was clearly written in the heavens at the moment he was born.

I could keep right on writing about the horoscopes of these great men, many of whom have been my clients in days gone by; but all I wish to do at this point is to emphasize the fact that what has been true in their cases is also true in yours. You may not have in your horoscope the very

same influences that the Prince of Wales has in his, or
Admiral Byrd in his. You may not be intended by the stars
to be a king on a throne or an explorer at the Pole, but
you have your own qualities, just as vital to you and—this
is the important thing—just as clearly defined in your chart!

TWELVE HUSBANDS

AND HOW TO TREAT THEM

You may have gathered from the two preceding chapters that it is my custom to follow the birthdays of important men and women in the public eye, and to consult their stars to see how closely they are living up to their horoscopes. It is a diversion for me. I do it in every spare moment, just as the postman, when he has a day off, goes for a walk!

But most people, I find, are naturally interested, first in their own stars, and then in those of the people with whom they are most closely associated. And they should be. For nothing contributes so much to happiness and success as knowing the "other fellow's" characteristics as well as you know your own. And nowhere is this more true than in the field of matrimony.

Fortunately, even the simplest form of astrological knowledge contributes in some measure to an understanding of this important matter. There are, for example, twelve types of husbands just as there are twelve signs of the Zodiac; and each type has his own peculiar characteristics, and should be treated in a different way.

Let's begin with Aries. Men born between March 22nd and April 20th come under this sign. They are natural knights and love to have their chivalry appealed to; they like to feel that they are, in some way, saving you and they love to fight for helpless women. They must continually be given a new thrill or supplied with a new surprise. They dislike to be tied down even to a budget, but prefer to be generous when they happen to be in the mood. When they have money they are often foolishly liberal, so purposely women should save a portion of what they give them in order that they may not be embarrassed when their funds are low.

Aries men are influenced by the cut of the hair and the hats you wear. They want women who can be companions and sports. But they want above all the pride of their sweethearts or wives. They like to make women feel that they are Sir Galahads; and the wise woman, therefore, will seem to appeal more to their pride and ambition than to their physical natures. Wives of Aries men should try to be popular with their husbands' men friends and they should be up to the minute in dress, manners, and in the news and topics of the day. But they should always remember that the Aries man is the adventurer, the leader, the pioneer. They should make him feel that he is blazing the trail and that they are following after.

But if they are married to a Taurian man—one born between April 21st and May 21st—their problem will be quite different. The Taurian man thrives on incessant attention. He is held by the physical things of life, by comfort and domesticity. It doesn't do for his wife to make his men friends like her too much. He would like to keep her in a harem. And she will get along with him best if she makes him feel that he is the only person in the world. In many matters, also, he is quite different from the Aries man. He likes to feel that his money has been wisely spent for practical matters connected with the home, especially features that add to his own comfort. He is particularly interested in the motherly qualities of the woman he has chosen for his wife. His highest ambition is to have a child to carry on his name. Wives of Taurian men, therefore, should lose no time in providing their husbands with offsprings of which they can be proud. If all else fails, they will be able to hold their husbands through the children whose interests they have in common.

Taurians are usually very sincere people with deep feeling and constant hearts, but they are often most exasperating husbands and lovers because they fail to do and say the nice things which mean so much in a woman's life. But this imperturbability is sometimes deceptive. Your average Taurian is patient and self-controlled, but if you goad him to a certain point he will break out in the most violent and injurious manner. Don't wave the red flag in front of the bull.

But the wife of a Taurus man has a comparatively simple job compared with the wife of a Gemini man. The latter is almost literally married to twins, to Castor and Pollux, perhaps even to Dr. Jekyll and Mr. Hyde. These men who are born between May 22nd and June 21st are usually brilliant, versatile, flexible, and changeable. Many of them are dilettante; a good many of them are flirts. Walt Whitman, who was a Gemini person, said of himself: "Do I contradict myself? Very well, I contradict myself. I am large. I contain multitudes." This is a typical Gemini man's opinion of himself; and frequently it is not far from right.

True family life does not appeal very strongly to a Gemini husband, but it is not distasteful to him. He acquiesces in the activities of the domestic circle without being moved either to intensity of affection or revolt. This is very true of most of his relations with humanity. To him human beings are only factors in his problems. He is not inclined to give himself to passionate expressions of affection nor does he appreciate them in others.

It is clear that the wife of a Gemini man is presented with a problem more social than amorous. She must possess unfailing adaptability to his changing moods. She must soothe his often turbulent mind. She must understand his unexpectedness, his many sudden deviations, and his often disconcerting agility. She must take his flirtations for what they are: flirtation. And she must get from him the mental stimulus which he is well fitted to give, for it is the mission of the Gemini person to stimulate, revive, refresh, to dig people out of ruts, and to keep the world eternally young. The Gemini man never grows up. He has many of the charms of a child, and he demands the same restrained tolerance a child demands.

When a Gemini man gets bored and upset with the world, as he is almost sure to do, he then says and does things which make people hate him if they do not understand that his condition is due to his peculiar horoscope and that it will be only a short time before he comes out of it. The unwise wife, at such a time, will argue with her husband. The wise wife will tell him he is the greatest man in the world.

Cancer men are more affectionate and sentiment-loving. They are always tender fathers and frequently protecting lovers, sensitive and sympathetic. In love the active type of Cancer man is tenacious, enduring, even self-sacrificing when his affections have once been fixed, although because of his normal good nature and desire to please, he may be accused of fickleness. The passive type is purely receptive. He accepts marriage as a settlement of life's problems and remains in it for the same reason. Usually they combine this love of tranquil domesticity with love of travel, of water, of beautiful scenery; they crave changing sensations and adventure. In their less charming moments they are apt to worry and be nervous, even fretful. They like to be reasonably economical except in matters of the table, where there is no limit to the money, time or energy they are willing to expend.

Here you have the thin-skinned, hyper-sensitive type of husband who suffers acutely from fancied slight. They must have congenial surroundings and associates who hold similar views on the essential aspects of life. They are dependent on sympathy and approval both in private and public relations. Discord or opposition tend to divert their best endeavors. Sympathy and patience are what they most need, and what they must have if they are to achieve the best results of which they are capable.

Wives should realize that underneath their changeableness and restlessness there is a great perseverance and tenacity of purpose which should be encouraged. These men are very easily influenced by those they love so long as they do not feel that they are being coerced. Intelligent non-resistance should be the slogan of the wife of any man born between June 22nd and July 23rd.

The quality of non-resistance is even more desirable in women who are married to natives of the masterful sign Leo which rules the destinies of people born between July 24th and August 23rd. Leo is the royal sign of the Zodiac and its natives are inclined to feel that they rule by divine right. The average son of Leo gets on well with his family because of his goodness of heart. In a sense he may be said to be domesticated, but he insists upon being the center of his domestic circle. His family must revolve around him. However humble his station in life he makes himself the king of a little court. When, as sometimes happens, the outside world refuses to cater to this desire for adulation, the Leo husband is apt to become a tyrant in his home circle. He expects everything to be done for him, not from laziness but from a desire to exercise his rights as he sees them.

In love he is the exact opposite of the Gemini man. His one thought is to give himself to the utmost. But even here his stress of his own value is so great that he often cannot conceive of any person refusing to accept the affection which he offers. However, he almost never harbors a grudge; and

underneath his show-off tendencies he possesses solid qualities of dependability, loyalty and generosity—a real sense of
noblesse oblige—to which the wise wife will appeal.

I am not going to tell you about all of these twelve husbands in such detail. If I did you would tire of them as
much as you might if you had to be married to all of them.
However, I do wish to give a brief description of each of
the other seven men so that you may know into which
classification your own husbands fall.

Do not expect anything thrillingly romantic from the
typical husband born between August 24th and September
23rd. Virgo men are more intellectual than emotional, but
they are excellent providers and, if the wife is not too
temperamental, make very satisfactory husbands. The
average Virgo man does not provoke trouble and does not
respond easily to it. He dislikes change and does not even
care to leave his home. He prefers the life of the village
or small town to that of the city. In love he talks the idea
of self-surrender; he does not even care much for the idea
of conquest; but his seeming indifference often makes him
popular with women, especially those who like to play at
love. His flirtations will usually be of a mild order, and
nothing is likely to occur to threaten the home.

A Libra husband—September 24th to October 23rd—is
one of the most difficult types for the average wife to understand. The native of Libra gets on very well in his home
owing to the charm of his manners and his general capacity
for doing things subtly without seeming to do them. He
has, however, no particularly strong or deep-rooted attach-
ment to his home; and though a break with his family is
comparatively rare, he does not possess the domestic sense
in anything like the same degree as the native of such signs
as Cancer or Taurus. His balanced nature gives him a very
good understanding of both the masculine and feminine atti-

tude toward love. For this reason he is apt to be an expert in all amorous matters. There is, however, nothing gross about the Libra husband. He is an artist in love. The Libra husband is the best of company, sociable, gay, often talented; but unless he is properly guided by a wise and tactful wife, he is likely to become a charming drifter, a beloved vagabond, a happy-go-lucky, who lives for and in the present. He is hopeless alone.

Scorpio which rules the period between October 24th and November 22nd, produces the most intensely passionate people of any sign in the Zodiac. The extreme type of Scorpio man is excessively jealous, inclined to be tyrannical, easy to offend, and revengeful when offended. His happiness depends on having a partner who is pliable, docile and patient. So long as everything goes his way, all right. Oppose him, and God help everybody! Highly developed Scorpio men like the late beloved Theodore Roosevelt turned this tremendous force into a passion for the hardest kind of work, for wild country, for physical prowess, and for clean living. The little girl who had a little curl must have been a Scorpio person because the natives of this sign when they are good are very good, but when they are bad they are horrid.

I can best illustrate the difference between the typical Sagittarius husband (November 23rd to December 22nd) and the typical Capricorn husband (December 23rd to January 20th) by retelling the story of an incident which happened in my early Boston experience as an astrologer. One of my most enthusiastic and faithful "believers" called me up to say that she must see me immediately. When I asked her what was the matter she answered: "Twins!" I was surprised for my friend was a maiden lady of long and respectable standing. But an astrologian learns to expect anything! So I told her to come and tell me all about it—

or them. Of course, the children weren't hers—but they were twins with only a few minutes' difference in their birth. I made out the two charts in accordance with this difference and began my reading with the remark:

"These two children are as unlike as if they had been born in different decades—one in India and the other in Sweden."

My caller gave a shout of triumph. You might have thought that she had just won a million dollar bet. As it turned out she had won a notable victory over her Back Bay physician, an old-timer who hadn't waked up to the value of astrology as an aid to medicine and the world. He had insisted that the science could not be true—and as final proof had offered these two babies, born almost at the same time, one as dark as the proverbial ace of spades and the other as fair as the queen of diamonds.

But "almost" is a big word. And in the case of these twins, it made all the difference in the world. At the moment of the birth of the older twin, the last degree of the fair complexion, happy disposition sign Sagittarius was rising, giving him the jovial beneficent optimistic planet Jupiter as his star of destiny. At the moment of the birth of the younger twin, the sign Capricorn—indicating a swarthy complexion and a serious disposition—was rising, giving him the melancholy Saturn as his dominant planet.

To an astrologian, the thing is as clear as black and white. Both children were born under signs with infinite possibilities for good, but they were as different as the symbols of those signs, the arrow and the goat; and they would require throughout their lives very different kinds of treatment from their chosen mates.

Not all Sagittarian men are blond; and not all Capricorn men are swarthy. However, most Sagittarius people are frank, outspoken, fearless, impulsive and direct; inherently unselfish, truthful and high-minded. A good many Capricorn men, on the other hand, are inclined to be too serious in temperament: self-conscious, introspective and fearful. Unless they are handled right, they tend to become materialistic, over-bearing, self-centered, and sometimes tyrannical. Qualities possessed by Aries and Leo women are naturally sympathetic to Sagittarians; and those which are characteristic of Taurus and Virgo women are peculiarly helpful to men born under Capricorn.

Aquarius is the birth sign of the optimist. Aquarians see things from a cosmic standpoint. They feel a universal rather than a personal love. The typical Aquarian is apt to be much more in love with a school, a hospital, or a science than he can ever be with an individual. However, when he does love, his genial amiability leads him to do all in his power to gratify the feelings of the other person. He respects himself and others, and expects them to respect both him and themselves. He can be relied upon not to quarrel unnecessarily or to do anything to break up an existing situation. He is inclined to be stronger in his friendships than in his loves; and it is on the intellectual and social side rather than on the sentimental side that the wise wife will make her appeal. Moreover, she must not be disturbed if her Aquarius-born husband (January 21st to February 19th) seems to broadcast the affection which a Cancer-born husband, for instance, would lavish exclusively on his family and home. The typical Aquarian is essentially a humanitarian.

Pisces, the twelfth sign of the Zodiac, rules the period from February 20th to March 21st, and is symbolized by the two fishes, one swimming upstream and one swimming down. In his relations with women the Pisces man is an exceptionally pleasing type. His devotion exceeds even that of Taurus, but is of a much more placid and soothing character. He has little tendency to infidelity of the active sort; but on the other hand, he does not offer so much resistance to the advances of the opposite sex as some jealous wives might wish. He is essentially a domesticated person. He does not give much active assistance in the home, but he always makes himself agreeable and is very often the pet of the family. Circumstances which irritate other people, do not affect him at all. He is a dreamer who may become a drifter. He dislikes competition, rivalry and warfare. He has the supersensitiveness of the artist and the poet. The sins of this sign are those of omission rather than commission. His ambition needs to be stimulated and his course held firm. He requires constant attention.

I must not leave you with the impression that these general remarks apply to *all* of the men born in these twelve periods. Do not condemn your husband, in fact do not take any unusual attitude whatsoever toward him, until you have more information than I can give you here as to the kind of man he is and the kind of treatment he should receive!

TWELVE WIVES

AND HOW THEY SHOULD BE TREATED

ONE woman's meat is another woman's poison. That is a statement which is abundantly proved by the different—and often strange—kinds of men that women choose for husbands. But it is a truth to which the husbands themselves give little thought. They fall into a certain husbandly formula for treating wives, and act on it blandly throughout their married lives, as if they believed that every woman was just like every other woman.

Of course she is not. And although it may be too much to ask of mere man that he understand woman in all her infinite variety, it would not seem too much to demand that he familiarize himself with the twelve basically different kinds of wives, and find out to which general division his own wife belongs.

For there are, as every astrologer knows, twelve kinds of wives corresponding to the twelve signs of the Zodiac. For example:

The Aries Wife
Born Between March 22nd and April 20th

Aries the Ram, the first of the twelve signs, stands for leadership, for ambition, for courage, for enthusiasm, for audacity. Obviously, a wife born under Aries' fiery, exciting and pioneering influence is a very different person from one born under Taurus the Bull or Scorpio the Scorpion.

If you, for instance, are a true daughter of Aries, you are

inclined to be a bit too aggressive. Your husband must exercise patience and tact in dealing with this tendency in order to preserve harmonious conditions in your home.

Your mind moves rapidly—sometimes too rapidly. You have natural executive ability, but to get the best results, you should be made to plan your work before you begin it. Your pioneer nature makes you a wonderful starter. Your husband should encourage you to be a good finisher.

You are generous. You despise anything mean or underhanded. You love practical achievement. But you are inclined to be critical, sometimes overbearing. Your husband must be very patient—or very firm—in dealing with this latter trait.

When Aries women fall in love, they become very romantic. They are given to violent, sudden enthusiasms. They do not care much for the routine of home-making. They do not create an atmosphere of rest, tranquillity, or serenity. These qualities do not belong to Aries the Ram.

If your husband was born under Leo or Sagittarius, he probably knows instinctively how to cope with your Aries tendencies. If not, he must learn through fore-warning or experience what must be obvious from this brief description: that the Aries wife must be handled with gloves!

The Taurus Wife
Born Between April 21st and May 21st

If you are like most daughters of Taurus, you are normally quiet and easy-going. When roused, however, you can be headstrong and wholly disregardful of consequences. Your husband, therefore, will do well not to rouse you!

So far as love is concerned, you and your husband should have few difficulties. Taurus is a warm, affectionate sign; and Venus, as a dominant influence, adds tremendously to your charm. Your chief trouble in this field will not come from your husband. It will arise from your own tendency to take too much for granted, or, rather to depend on others taking too much for granted. If you love someone, tell him so; not once, but every day.

From the position of the Sun when you were born, I should say that your most congenial mates might be found among men born under Virgo or Capricorn. If your husband was not born under either of these especially congenial signs, he must cultivate congeniality on his own hook.

The characteristics of your sign which your husband must bear always in mind are a persistence which sometimes amounts to obstinancy, a conservatism which verges on unadaptability, and a strong will which may degenerate into argumentativeness

You are extremely fond of all kinds of comforts and luxuries. You love domesticity—your babies and everything to do with your home. You are strongly emotional. And you should be. For your finest qualities are an outgrowth of full emotional life.

And your husband must make sure that you get it. If he hopes to hold your affections and make you happy, he should contrive to keep a comfortable roof over your head and a cuddly baby in your arms!

The Gemini Wife
Born Between May 22nd and June 21st

Gemini is the astrological sign which rules the United States, and if you are a daughter of Gemini, you probably possess that quality which is most characteristic of your fellow countrymen: versatility.

As a wife, this is your strength and your weakness. Variety is the breath of life to you, but you must be made to cultivate stick-to-it-iveness to keep the breath of life *in* you. You will be divided between a desire to stand by your husband and a desire to walk out on him. He must see that you stand by him.

Extreme versatility, a highly developed mentality, and an over-sensitive nature are usually accompanied by an over-supply of nerves, and as a result, Gemini women too often suffer from neuritis. And their husbands must be prepared to suffer, too!

You are not a born home-maker, but you love to have comfort and beauty about you. You provide a charming background for romance. You have a gift for affection. Use it. But your husband must see to it that you use it only on him.

Your sign is symbolized by the Twins—and from this fact, your husband, if he is wise, should take warning as to one way to cure your tendency to dissipate your energies. He should encourage you to carry along two kinds of work at the same time. Thus, he may satisfy your desire for change, which is the curse of the Gemini tribe.

If your husband is a Libra or Aquarius person, he will probably know instinctively how to handle you. If not, he should read this book!

The Cancer Wife
Born Between June 22nd and July 23rd

Cancer rules the city of New York. And its daughters, like the women of our gay metropolis, are always ready for a new experience. Their husbands, if they are wise, will keep their minds and their hours well occupied.

If you are a true daughter of Cancer, you are a lover of travel, adventure, romance and the occult. At the same time, you will hold fast to traditions of the past, and will hesitate to cut yourself off from familiar surroundings, you will not wish to leave your family—especially your children. Your husband should make a cult of domesticity.

Your interest in good things to eat will turn you towards dietetics, chemistry and domestic science. Your love of home will make you a good home-maker. Your love of children will bring you success in any activity connected with their welfare. Your husband cannot go wrong through encouraging these tendencies.

Cancer is the sign of motherhood. Women born in this sign usually long for children, but sometimes care little about marriage. It is possible that the strong influence of the Moon in your horoscope may lead you into some such attitude, and I strongly advise your husband to guard against it. Your intensely loyal disposition demands a husband on whom to lavish your affections, and he should help you to remember that grown-up boys need a good deal of mothering—and what's more, they like it.

Your most congenial mates—marital or otherwise—are likely to be found among men born under Scorpio or Pisces!

The Leo Wife
Born Between July 24th and August 23rd

You were born under the royal sign of the Zodiac. And like most people born to the purple, you feel that you rule by divine right. Your husband, if he is wise, will accept this fact philosophically, and will content himself with encouraging you to use your power for the common good.

His task should not be difficult. For as a true daughter of Leo you are naturally high-minded. You possess a well-developed sense of noblesse oblige. You are generous, sometimes to the point of extravagance. You are an untiring worker, but dislike menial tasks. You are impatient of routine. You possess rare executive ability. You can be a leader in any group or community. Your husband cannot expect you to confine your activities to the home.

But love is your real kingdom. You are capable of the highest devotion to those you love: of an adoration which amounts to worship. You may be hurt by the inability of some people to respond in either kind or degree; but on the other hand, the generosity and abandon of your love may rouse the same qualities and give you the response which your warm, affectionate nature craves. Your husband must be your lover, too.

Your most congenial marriage partners may be found under Sagittarius or Aries.

Your husband should be warned that in love you give yourself to the limit, but that you are easily wounded. Your pride as well as your heart is hurt. You love to be loved, and you love to have others see that you are loved. You give everything—and expect much. The husband of a Leo woman has his work cut out for him!

The Virgo Wife
Born Between August 24th and September 23rd

The ruling planet of your sign is Mercury. And since Mercury rules the intellect, your husband must help you to live up to the opportunities for mental development which the stars have given you.

Like most daughters of Virgo, you have a keen eye for detail. You love to study a problem and to solve it by some device or system of your own. You are great on devices and systems! Your husband mustn't let you follow this tendency too far; it will complicate your own life and burden his.

Most mentalities are not so dexterous as your own. Your husband should try to keep you from talking too much about your own ideas. They are more important to you than to anyone else. And men don't like women who talk about themselves. They reserve that privilege for their own sex!

The chief faults of your sign with which your husband may have to contend are a tendency to be overcritical, a failure to express the appreciation of others which you often feel, a slowness to forgive which is the natural counterpart of your slowness to anger, and a tendency to keep too much to yourself.

Perhaps a husband born under Capricorn or Taurus would be best fitted to bring out your good points. But whatever sign he is born under, he should persuade you to present a more "social" side to the world. It will increase your popularity with both sexes, and your chances of happiness in your married life.

Above all, your husband should urge you to be less critical —to remember his good points, and forget his bad!

The Libra Wife
Born Between September 24th and October 23rd

When it comes to love—and it usually does come to it, doesn't it?—you daughters of Libra have the most interesting temperament of all the natives of the Zodiac. Love should be an important element in your life, and rightly so. You have a great understanding of the masculine temperament.

On the other hand, you tend to create an image which you worship as the heathen does his idol. This may cause you some disappointment, because there are few human beings worthy of such idealization. Your husband should do his best not to let these disappointments shadow your life.

You are willing to grant a good deal of personal liberty to the man you love, but you must not be surprised if he is not willing to grant the same amount to you. However, your husband if he is wise will overcome some of his masculine prejudices on this point.

Your most congenial marriage partners are likely to be found among Aquarius or Gemini men. Your husband must remember that as a daughter of Libra, you love beauty, harmony, symmetry, justice. You exemplify in your nature the Scales, which are the symbol of this sign. You have the finest sensibilities. You recoil from the crude; you tend naturally toward the exquisite.

Your husband should encourage you either to engage in the arts yourself, or to enrich your life by an appreciation of them; for you will find your greatest happiness in association with artistic people.

In short, he should bend every effort to surround you with people and things which will bring beauty and harmony into your life; and his!

The Scorpio Wife
Born Between October 24th and November 22nd

Scorpio has two symbols, the Scorpion and the Eagle. And it is fitting that it should be so; for there is as much difference between the lowest and the highest type of Scorpio woman as there is between the lowly Scorpian and the soaring Eagle. Your husband should know which kind of Scorpio wife he is married to!

He should realize that you face great opportunities and great dangers. He should help you to mobilize the unusual abilities which your sign gives you, to enable you to seize the former and avoid the latter. He must be careful not to let the force of your impulsive nature lead you into indiscretion and excess.

Your most congenial mates, everything else being equal, are likely to be born under Pisces or Cancer.

Your husband's problem is simplified by the fact that you are a one-man woman. You feel very strongly toward the person you love, but you appear cold and indifferent to others. However, he must try to keep you from becoming attracted to your inferiors or people in lower stations in life. If he doesn't, you may find yourself involved in strange and destructive love affairs.

You are very magnetic, and have a strong physical appeal for men. You are likely to stir the passions of your admirers to the apparent exclusion of higher sentiments. To counteract this fact by making your magnetism operative on a higher plane is your main job in life. To keep his feelings for you on that high plane is your husband's!

The Sagittarius Wife
Born Between November 23rd and December 22nd

If you are a true daughter of Sagittarius, you should be popular with your own circle and successful with the crowd. Your husband should be wise enough to know that all you need to do to gain both of these objectives is to curb your tendency to blunt speech and brusqueness of manner, which scare a good many away. Your husband should strive to thicken up his skin.

You are inclined to be nervous, high-strung, over-sensitive. Your feelings are easily injured. Your impulsiveness sometimes reacts upon yourself. You drop the thing you are doing before it is finished. Your husband, if he is wise, will help you to school yourself to patience and tenacity. He will encourage you to hitch your wagon to a star, but he won't let you forget to tie the rope.

I don't mean that he should try to make a plodder out of you. He must realize that you are the kind that has flashes of inspiration. Call it feminine intuition, clairvoyance or simply "hunch"—you have it. And it will prove the greatest factor in your happiness. He should encourage you to have faith in this quality, but not to become a slave to stray impulses.

If your husband is the Aries or Leo type he will probably be sufficiently congenial not to mind your tendency to brusqueness. In any case, he must remember that you are the breezy type of lover rather than the romantic. Your men are pals, comrades, chums. You demand many friendships outside the family circle. Personal freedom is your dominant passion. This might cause you some difficulties if you were married to a man who was either very romantic or very jealous. But of course *your* husband isn't that way!

The Capricorn Wife
Born Between December 23rd and January 20th

You have strong domestic instincts. You love anniversaries and family gatherings of all sorts. You attach the greatest importance to marriage, but your husband must help you to exercise finesse in order to make a success of it. Both you and he should strive to keep your affections on a spiritual plane.

According to the position of the Sun in your horoscope, your most congenial life partners may be found among Virgo or Taurus men.

If you are a true daughter of Capricorn, you are a born worker. Your energy is tireless, your ambition insatiable. You long for power. You value both knowledge and wealth for the power they give you. You attract friends in high places. You get your share of the world's favors. You are surrounded by rivals, but you prevail over them. Your husband must realize that he is dealing with a positive force.

However, underneath your self-assertive manner, there is

sometimes a foreboding of evil which mars your happiness and hinders your success. For one thing, it may make you thrifty almost to the point of penuriousness. Your husband must set you an example both of courage and generosity.

In love there is a danger that you may become self-centered, giving too little attention to the other person's side of the equation. All your instincts are of the healthiest sort, but you do not pay as much attention as you should to the niceties of romance.

Your husband should help you to develop the finer, softer side of your nature, to guard against a tendency to lack of sympathy and pride, and to take life no more seriously than it takes you!

The Aquarius Wife
Born Between January 21st and February 19th

Your husband is fortunate in the fact that you were born in one of the best signs of the Zodiac. You are naturally of a humanitarian nature. Your great pleasure is to do good to others. You see the world whole. You rise above personal desires and selfish aims.

You have it in you to make a loyal wife and a highly successful mother. You would also excel as a teacher, writer, social worker, or nurse. You might even become interested in astronomy, astrology, and occult research. You possess an intuition which is akin to prophecy. In fact, it is often taken for prophecy. Your husband must never forget that he is only your husband—that you belong to the whole world.

Your husband does not need to warn you against sloth or changefulness. You work hard and to the end. Your success is won that way. It is not the overnight kind. It comes slowly, but it lasts. You are any man's equal—and know it. Your husband may as well understand that fact.

In love affairs you are essentially loyal and devoted, but inclined to be undemonstrative. You are so interested in the world in general that you may seem to neglect the man you love. Your husband must help you to guard against this tendency, and he probably will! Men like to feel that they come first in the mind and heart of the woman they love.

Husbands born under Gemini or Libra are especially successful in dealing with Aquarius wives. But any man who truly loves you can achieve happiness with you if he is himself sufficiently unselfish and disinterested—if he never forgets that you are first of all a humanitarian, that the universe is more important to you than any one person in it!

The Pisces Wife
Born Between February 20th and March 21st

Being a daughter of Pisces, you are naturally sensitive, sympathetic, intuitive and agreeable. You make an excellent companion; a pleasing, comfortable, lovable mate. You have high ideals and fine feelings.

From the position of the sun when you were born, I should say that your most congenial mates might be found among men born under Cancer or Scorpio. But no matter which sign your husband was born under, one of his first duties should be to bolster up your self-confidence—to convince you of your ability to do anything you start out to do. Above all, he should urge you to concentrate. You are interested, or should be, in artistic and æsthetic things.

If your husband finds that you are apt to go first one way and then another like the symbol of your sign—the two fishes swimming in opposite directions—he must not blame you or himself. All that he can do is to help you to make up your mind that you will swim upstream, and only upstream.

You are generous to a fault. You are a great lover of beauty in both nature and art. You are impressionable and intuitive, but inclined to lack logic and consistency. You can be stubborn and rather trying at times. But your husband must not lose sight of the fact that your great unselfishness should offset these tendencies and make you a most desirable wife for the right sort of man.

Your greatest crosses are apt to come through your affections, because you are so unselfish yourself that you will naturally expect the same quality in others. Also, your naturally demonstrative nature may be rebuffed by an apparent failure to respond or the part of the person you love. Let us hope that your husband is the responsive kind!

And Wives in General

I have described twelve types of wives and have tried to give a few hints as to how they should be treated. But I don't pretend to have described *all* the different kinds of wives there are. Astrology teaches that every person is different from every other person. Especially women! And for this reason I should warn you that not everything I have said necessarily applies to *you* in every detail. If I knew the year and day and hour you were born as well as the month, I might find something in your individual horoscope which would make you different in many vital respects from all the other women in your sign.

So, if your husband reads this chapter, and finds that you are not a perfect Aries wife or a perfect Taurus wife or a perfect Capricorn wife, don't let him find fault with you for that. Few people in this world are perfect—even wives!

WHAT ASTROLOGY IS NOT

SOME POPULAR MISCONCEPTIONS

HISTORIANS and archæologists have proved beyond the shadow of doubt that during the periods of greatest human enlightenment, astrology was studied and accepted by the wisest and most influential people of ancient times—the kings, the philosophers, the generals, the statesmen.

Even in the Middle Ages, as you have seen if you have toured the château country of France, the astrologer's chamber was always next in position and second in importance to that of the feudal lord of the castle.

Cardinal Richelieu was a great believer in astrology. It was said that he collected the horoscopes of all the kings and princes in Europe, and at the height of his power never granted audiences without first consulting their charts. In all ages, astrology has entered into the councils of princes and guided the policy of kings.

And the situation today is not so greatly different from that which has always existed so far as it concerns the great man's dependence on his stars. I have told you elsewhere of some of my own famous clients of the years gone by—of James J. Hill and Lillian Nordica and Enrico Caruso and J. Pierpont Morgan and John Burroughs and King Edward VII—and the records in my personal files of men and women who are alive today show that the same condition still exists. If I were at liberty to tell you the names of the famous men and women who consult me today in my studio, I could give you a list as notable as those found on the old Egyptian monuments from which we get our earliest knowledge of astrology's place in the annals of mankind.

Yet there is no subject about which there is less accurate, authentic information in printed form. So, in order to clear up some of the popular misconceptions in regard to the science, I have selected a few of the questions, which have been most frequently asked me during my thirty-five years in astrology, and will try to answer them once for all in these pages.

The first and—to an astrologer—the most trying of these questions is this one: *"Does astrology teach fatality?"*

No. We are not tied to the wheels of destiny. We are in this life to help the wheels go round—to help the stars help us. Astrology, in my opinion, must be right. There can be no appeal from the Infinite. But the horoscope does not pronounce sentence. It places mankind on probation. It gives warning. It points out the good along with the bad. It shows how to offset the latter with the former. It shows tendencies rather than deeds. Tendencies may be unavoidable; but deeds are what the individual makes them. They vary according to man's success in overcoming bad tendencies and strengthening good ones. Man can be the master of his fate! The fool thinks he rules his stars, the wise man co-operates with them.

And that is why, in all my work, from interviews with private clients to the Solar Horoscopes which are a part of this book, I never talk about fatality, I never let the individual feel that there is anything so unfavorable in his horoscope that he cannot, by knowledge, conquer it. I tell the bad tendencies along with the good, but I always show how these bad tendencies can be overcome. Astrology does not take from you the God-given right of free will, but strengthens that free will and shows you how you can use it to maximum advantage for yourself and for the world.

These questions about fatality always sadden me. For example, I received this one from a woman whose discouraged plight pulled right at my heart strings: "Dear Miss Adams: Please explain why the 12th of May is such an unlucky date. All the women who have this birth date seem to be born to ill-health. They all have trouble in their parents' home. They all seem to marry badly and live in desperate poverty. Their friends all try to see who can do them the most harm. Please tell me, dear Miss Adams, how they may attract money and proper social standing. Is Saturn their evil star? Must they be unfortunate right to the grave?" The answer to this question is, of course, *"Absolutely not!"* There is no such thing as a universally unfortunate birth date, for the very good reason that no two days—certainly not two May 12ths—are alike.

I recall another letter which takes up another phase of this same subject, which began: "Dear Miss Adams: Would you help some persons very much interested in astrology by stating whether, in all your long experience, you have ever come on an absolutely and entirely afflicted chart? A very dear friend of mine, a woman, consulted an astrologer who told her that she had nothing whatever to hope for as long as she lived. It is true that my friend has had unusually hard luck—her hard luck having apparently even pursued her only son. But what my friends and I cannot understand is that if the planets move in their course they should show only their malefic side to some persons. If the astrologer was correct, then the belief in God as a Loving Father is erroneous, isn't it?" The astrologer was *not* correct—not in a million years! I have never seen an absolutely afflicted horoscope, and never has anybody else, because there is no such thing. When the poet said that there is so much bad in the best of us and so much good in the worst of us that it hardly behooves any of us to talk about the rest of us (I am quoting from memory), he not only voiced a great social truth, but he recorded a great spiritual one. There *is* bad in the best of us and there *is* good in the worst of us. And no one knows that better—at least no one *should* know it better—than an astrologer.

The question, "How about Pluto?" in the "Now—we've caught you" from which it usually comes to me is too ridiculous to notice, but the fact that it is asked at all, shows that there is a real curiosity as to how this latest discovery will affect the calculations of astrology.

Some unthinking people assume that it knocks out the science altogether: that all our previous calculations must be wrong. Of course, nothing could be farther from the truth. The astrologer works, just as the astronomer works, with the material at hand. Before Neptune and Uranus were discovered, both based their calculations on the fire planets they then knew. What Neptune and Uranus did to astrology was to supply new data; they didn't change the old. And that is what this new planet will do. When we have had a chance to study it over a period of years and to learn its influence on our lives by observation and experiment, we will know just that much more about ourselves than we did before. Our knowledge will be that much more "refined." Our science will be that much more "exact." And so will the astronomer's. The more accurate their science becomes, the more accurate ours will be. We welcome their aid. It is too bad that they do not more often welcome ours—because, in the words of Coleridge, "there is no doubt about it but that astrology of some sort or another will be the last achievement of astronomy."

And now for a question of procedure: *"Is it any advantage in preparing a horoscope to see the subject?"*

Absolutely not! If anything it is a disadvantage, because it allows the personality of the person who needs help to come between me and the mathematical calculations from which that help must come. People tell me that, when they come into my studio, I do not look at them. Some are even offended because of this fact. But I don't mean to be impolite. I might be delighted to meet them socially; in fact, many of my closest friends have come to me through the medium of my astrological practice; but, scientifically speaking, I do not care during the first minutes of an interview whether my caller is blonde or brunette, short or tall, light as a feather or heavy as a rock. All I wish to know is when and where he or she was born—facts which I immediately write in the hub of the wheel-like chart on which I draw the horoscope. That is why people have written to me from every corner of the star-lit globe and have received through the mail the same help and comfort and solace they would have received if they had been sitting in my studio.

Another question which is frequently asked me is "What is the theory of vibrations on which astrology is based?"

One correspondent puts it this way: "What is this theory of vibrations you are always talking about? Why don't you give us the scientific explanation of it, so we can judge for ourselves?" Well, I *will!* A vibration, according to Webster's New International Dictionary, is a term in physics meaning "a periodic motion of the particles of an elastic body or medium in alternately opposite directions from the position of equilibrium."

There! Do you know any more than you did before? I am frank to say I don't get enough out of a scientific definition of that sort (without a great deal of careful study) to justify including it as a general thing in my astrological writings. The very people who reproach me for not making my explanations more scientific would be the first to close their books if I fed them on phrases like "alternately opposite directions from the position of equilibrium." They would think I had lost my *own* equilibrium—mental as well as physical!

No, I prefer the more human explanation which my dear old friend and client, John Burroughs, gave me when I asked him the basis of his belief in astrology. "Miss Adams," he said, "I have found in my work that everything in nature influences everything else, so why shouldn't the stars influence man?"

There, Mr. Skeptic! Have I answered your question without going too far into technicalities? I hope so, because I always prefer to discuss astrology in terms of everyday life. But for the benefit of those who are seriously interested in the scientific basis of astrology, I would like to make a few comparisons which may prove comforting.

The very day I received that letter demanding a "scientific explanation" of how the stars affect man, I opened my morning paper and read this headline: "Find. Moon Affects Speed of Clocks: Yale Scientists at Meeting of Astronomers Tell of Study Made with Loomis Chronograph." Then followed this account: "The most precise check ever made on the world's most accurate clocks was described by Dr. E. W. Brown of Yale University, president of the American Astronomical Society, when that organization met here today for a three-day session. A striking fact brought out by the study is that the pendulums of the clocks are pulled first one way, then the other, by the Moon. The gravitational attraction of the Moon pulls the pendulum toward it, so when it is rising in the East they are pulled in a different direction from that when the Moon sets in the West. This causes the clock to go slightly faster or slower in a period of about twelve and a half hours. In this time the clock gains or loses fifteen hundred thousandths of a second."

If one set of scientists can calculate down to *fifteen hundred thousandths of a second* the effect of a heavenly body on a man-made metal contraption like a clock, isn't it rea, sonable that another set of scientists working with the same kind of data, can calculate the effect of that same body on man himself?

You may say that astronomy is a different kind of science from astrology. It is. But not a younger one or a less adequately proven one. Who can explain to your satisfaction or mine why the Moon traveling through the heavens should affect a clock on your living room mantel? Scientists can't and they don't try to. All they know is that they have been watching this and similar actions for thousands of years and have found them to be true. Nobody knows the *why* of these things. But after they have happened *often* enough, they are accepted as so. A "natural law" is established.

The law of gravitation is such a law. Sir Isaac Newton lying under a tree and noticing the apple fall to the ground didn't make gravitation a law; but thousands of other cases, watched and tested because of the theory which he first advanced, have *proven* it to be a law. Now, it is the same way with astrology, only its array of tested and proven cases goes back centuries before Sir Isaac Newton was born. In fact, its records for accuracy go back further than those of *any* other science.

Take chemistry, for instance. It isn't so very long ago that a chemist was considered a black magician. Now we accept the fact that certain electrons combine to form oxygen and that others combine to form hydrogen. We know that oxygen and hydrogen in certain proportions combine to form water. We know this because the facts have been observed thousands of times under all sorts of different conditions; and we are agreed that what we call a "natural law" always functions the same way when the same conditions exist, and water is the result. So, in astrology, we know from thousands of accurately recorded observations made in the true spirit of science that certain combinations of planetary influences will produce certain effects. But neither the chemist nor the astrologer knows *why* these things are so any more than a biologist knows why a seed grows when it is planted and watered, or why a puppy grows up to be a dog!

If you keep a closed mind on this important subject, if, for example, you accept astronomy and do not accept astrology, that is, as the boys say, "your hard luck." In so doing, you are not only depriving yourself of invaluable help in managing your daily life, but you are going contrary to some of the greatest philosophers and scientists of all time. Lord Bacon, it was, the most intellectual man of his time, who said: "The knowledge of the actual motions of the heavenly bodies Socrates considers of little value. The appearances which make the sky beautiful at night are, he tells us, like the figures which a geometrician draws on the sand, mere examples, mere helps to feeble minds. *We must get beyond them.* We must attain to astronomy which is as independent of the actual stars as geometrical truth is independent of the lines of a badly drawn diagram." And, in our own country, almost in our own time, the greatest philosopher America has produced, Ralph Waldo Emerson, voices the same thought. "Astronomy," says Emerson, "is excellent, but *it must come down into life* to have its full value, and not remain there in globes and spaces."

"Down into life!" That's a great phrase. That's what astrology does. That's what this astrologer, in these pages, is trying to do. And when I get critical letters, as I sometimes do, from cranks who say I am not being true to the traditions of astrology in talking of it in such simple terms as the ones I use, I say "Bosh!" Libraries of learned, "highbrow" books have been written on every subject under the sun, but it is the simple book that everybody can understand which has the real influence.   Statesmen and scholars thundered through the years about the evils of slavery, but it was "Uncle Tom's Cabin" that brought the black man's freedom! Philosophers from Socrates down have discoursed on the virture of public and private honesty, but it took Theodore Roosevelt to sum it all up in one phrase, that we can never forget: "The Square Deal!"

I don't hope to be as successful as these great minds have been.   I haven't the gift of epigram or of narrative.   But if I can explain astrology to you so that you can understand it, without confusing your mind with talk about transits and ascendants and descendants and lunar mansions, I shall feel that this "popular" book on astrology has fulfilled its stars.

There is no more room in this already long chapter for other frequently asked questions, but there is one subject ever on the lips of skeptics which deserves and shall receive a chapter by itself.   That subject is "Twins!"

TWINS, TRIPLETS, QUADRUPLETS, DOUBLES

DO THEY PROVE ASTROLOGY OR DISPROVE IT?

WHENEVER an item appears in the papers recording some unusual feature of the lives—or deaths—of people born at the same time, I am deluged with letters. I recall especially the huge mail which followed a story about a father and mother who came from a hospital where they had left one twin son seriously injured by a fall to find that the other twin had just been run over by a truck. Most of the letters pointed to this sad event as absolute proof of the truth of astrology; but others pointed with equal conviction to twins of their acquaintance who had led widely differing lives. There seemed to be an unending interest in the problem.

Frequently, the items sent me by my twin-minded correspondents are of a more humorous variety. I well remember one clipping from a western paper sent me by a faithful follower. "Albert and Herman Jackson," the clipping read, "were Chicago twins. In 1926 they married twin sisters. In 1929, they had another double wedding, again marrying twin sisters. Brought into court charged with bigamy, the judge couldn't tell either husbands or wives apart. Finally, in desperation, he demanded that Albert Jackson take his two wives and stand at one side of the court room, and Herman take his two and go to the other side. They followed instructions, which the judge took as prima facie evidence that they were guilty of bigamy, and sentenced them to jail accordingly. It was a tight place for the judge but he pulled out of it with flying colors!"

Yes, twins always have their humorous aspects. But for those who are seriously concerned about this problem and its relation to astrology—and I am convinced that there are many such—I am going to analyze in this chapter some of the more interesting cases which have come under my observation, and show you how they prove rather than disprove astrology's infallibility.

It is true, according to astrology's teaching, that two people born at the same time, and in the same place, should look alike and act alike and encounter similar destinies. And as a matter of fact, it usually happens that way, even when twins are born several minutes apart. But it doesn't *necessarily* happen that way. In the few minutes that intervene between the birth of one twin and the birth of the other, the planetary conditions in the heavens *may* change radically.

I tell elsewhere in these pages the case of the twins in Boston, one light-complexioned and jovial, the other swarthy and solemn. This difference was due to the fact that the first twin *happened* to be born when the very last degree of the sign Sagittarius was rising in the heavens, and the second twin happened to be born when the Sagittarius influence had passed and the sign Capricorn was beginning to be in the ascendant. You Sagittarius and Capricorn people can tell, if you look at your Solar Horoscope in Part I of this book, just how the change in the heavens might affect these two children.

But it is not always a difference in the signs which causes these exceptions to the general rule. Sometimes it is a difference in planets. I had an extreme example several years ago of the effect of Uranus on an individual horoscope in the case of twin boys, born within fifteen minutes of each other in the city of St. Louis, who developed very different personalities. One was very, very good, and the other was horrid! Upon investigation, I found that this was one of those rare astrological freaks where one child was born on one side of the planetary fence and the other, after the passage of only a few minutes, was born on the other side. Uranus, which causes children to display contrary and rebellious characteristics, ruled one boy and the jovial beneficent Jupiter ruled the other. With this knowledge, I was able to give the mother of those twins worth-while advice as to how to deal with the two temperaments, especially that of the "bad" one, who really wasn't bad at all but merely required special treatment to deal with his Uranian tendencies.

The thing to remember, however, is that it is a rare thing to run across twins who *happened* to be born at such crucial times. Most twins are born under similar astrological conditions, and have, therefore, similar destinies. When one of them is under accidental conditions, the other is, too. And, doubtless, that was the case with the brothers who met with accidents at the same time.

And, of course, everything which has been said about twins applies also to triplets. A friend of mine once sent me a clipping from a New England newspaper which carried this arresting headline: "One Triplet Born Last Month. Other Two Today. A Mile Removed." Here is the story, verbatim: "The birth of triplets is a rare occurrence. And when the births occur at widely separated places, it is rarer still. But Newburyport has triplets that were born in two different months! Last night at 11:15 the stork visited Mrs. Oscar Eaton, 39 year old mother of seven children at her home, 7 Cedar Street. That was in November and the new visitor was a boy. (The clipping, you have probably gathered, was dated December 1st.) This morning about one o'clock in December—a girl was born to Mrs. Eaton. Then, about an hour afterward, the third birth occurred and was a boy. The last two were born at the Anna Jaques Hospital, more than a mile from the place where the first was born, and from which the mother had in the meantime been removed. All are doing nicely, thank you!"

Well, that was a remarkable thing, whatever way you looked at it. One of the triplets was born at home and two in a hospital. One will celebrate his birthday on November 30th, and the other two on December 1st. The case intrigued me, and I think it may you. Of course, the difference in place didn't make any special difference astrologically—a mile was too short a distance to reckon with in the vastness of the universe—but the question naturally arose: "Will the boy who was born on the last day of November be different from the brother and sister born on the first day of December?"

The answer is that he will, radically. Of course, all three will have many traits in common. Each was born while the Sun was in the direct, open, brilliant sign Sagittarius, and since the Sun is the most important factor in determining character, there is every reason to believe that they will have many similar characteristics. Moreover, all three children have planets in the house ruling brothers and sisters—which is fair enough, since the Eaton family has now reached the healthy total of six boys and four girls!

All three also have what we astrologers call an afflicted Moon, meaning that they should be on their guard all their lives against misfortunes through women. I suppose the cynical among you will say that there must be a lot of afflicted Moons floating around in men's horoscopes! And there *are*. But simply because there is a warning of trouble from this source does not mean that there will be such trouble. Astrology's job is to issue warnings before events rather than lamentations after it. Fore-warned is fore-armed. Fore-knowledge is power—usually it is safety.

But to get back to the triplets: although all of their Moons are afflicted, the first one's is afflicted in quite a different way from the other two. In his case, it is up to the mother to see that she does not misunderstand him or even in her love become too exacting. In the case of the other two, the danger from women, both with the boy and the girl, is some way connected with marriage. The boy may suffer through picking the wrong mate; the girl through the jealousy of another woman.

But the main difference between the November 30th horoscope and the December 1st ones is that in the former, Jupiter, the most powerful planet in the heavens, is in the house of friends, indicating that his greatest good fortune will come through *others;* whereas in the horoscopes of the other two, Jupiter is in the midheaven, indicating that their success will come because of their *own* character and their *own* efforts.

Not long after this case of the New England triplets, an even more amazing instance of quadruplets came to me from an old client, a judge in Pennsylvania, who noted with glee that the four girls were born in the sign Gemini, symbolized by the Twins!

That was true: they were all born on June 4th, almost in the middle of the sign Gemini, which is, as you probably know, a highly mental sign ruled by Mercury. This accounted for many qualities and characteristics which they had in common: the high scholarship which you would expect from daughters of Mercury, the God of the Mind, and the versatility which is the outstanding trait of the Gemini-born. It did not account, however, for certain differences which I noted the moment I looked at the newspaper pictures which the judge sent me. These differences so aroused my curiosity that I wrote to the mother of the four girls, Mrs. F. M. Keyes of Hollis, Oklahoma, asking her to send me the exact hour of birth of each child.

Mrs. Keyes answered my inquiry with a most cordial letter

saying that all four were born between midnight and 1 A.M. I wrote back and said in effect that I didn't see how this could be, because Pisces, the sign which was rising during all of that particular hour could hardly have produced a child with a face and expression like that of Leota, one of the four girls. "Her type," I wrote the mother, "is so different that the only explanation would seem to be that she was born either just before midnight or considerably afterward."

Mrs. Keyes' second letter gave the exact hour and minute for each girl. And it was just as I thought: Leota was *not* born in the hour between twelve and one! The first three *were*—and they looked it, excellent Pisces types, so much alike that a stranger could not tell them apart. Leota was born between one and two, well after the other three were safely in the world, and *when the pioneer sign Aries, the sign of leadership, was rising in her chart.*

"You seem to be quite curious," Mrs. Keyes wrote in her second letter, "about Leota. She *is* very different from the other girls in a number of things. In the first place, she is a blonde while the others are brunettes. Moreover, she is a ruler, and seems to have a lot of executive ability." There you are! The Aries gift of leadership. The Aries power to command. The Aries trait of executive ability. And the Aries tendency to blondeness! You see, you can't get away from your stars—even if you are a quadruplet!

So far as astrology is concerned, everything which applies to children born into one family applies equally well to children born into different families at the same time and in the same place. In this connection I wish to quote from an interesting article by Edwin T. Woodall, the former Scotland Yard detective, who acted as bodyguard to His Majesty, Edward VII. "One of the most vivid and hilariously funny memories of King Edward," writes Mr. Woodall, "is the story of William Hayes, the living image of the King. At that time, there was a certain hostess in London who was the incarnation of the spirit of the society climber. She had tried every conceivable way of penetrating court circles, and had failed. So, perhaps for spite, maybe because she was naturally indiscreet, she put in circulation a series of unsavory, waspish stories about the King and his friends.

"The King stood it for a while, but when the offense was repeated, this time involving a lady of spotless reputation, he decided to punish the offender. The ambitious hostess soon received a letter which gave her the thrill of her life. It was an intimation that the King, himself, would dine at her house on a certain night." When the night came, Mr. Woodall was waiting in the King's antechamber to accompany His Majesty to a dinner at the French Embassy. "I got the shock of my life," he says, "when someone looking exactly like the King, wearing the 'garter' and a star, and accompanied by a young equerry, emerged from the King's apartments, while the King himself, similarly dressed, stood in the doorway laughing as he watched the other depart. Which was the King?"

Well, you can guess the rest: how William went to the ambitious lady's dinner and Edward went to the Embassy. What happened at the latter function is not chronicled. But what happened at my lady's dinner party was as follows: The bogus King Edward not only attended the feast and fooled everybody, including men and women who knew the King well, but he got gloriously drunk, kissed all the girls, sang ribald songs, and behaved himself generally in such an offensive manner that someone telephoned Buckingham Palace to send someone around to take the King home!

A more decorous instance is recorded by St. John, a distinguished writer on the occult. "Many years ago," he writes, "there came to me an old clergyman; he said he did not wish

to have his character read, but to know if I had any reasonable proof of the truth of my science. After I had shown
him my examples, and he had professed himself satisfied, he
surprised me by saying that he was himself a proof of the
truth of astrology. It seemed that he and another little
boy had been born almost simultaneously in their village in
Wales

At the age of sixty, the clergyman went back in search
of his contemporary twin, and, seated in a hut in the Welsh
hills together they went through the history of their lives.
It appeared that they grew up very much alike in temperament and in time the clergyman became a shepherd of souls,
the poor boy a shepherd of sheep. Both remained in mod-
erate circumstances; both enjoyed the same good health; such
illnesses as they suffered occurred at exactly the same date.

They each married, in the same year, a woman of the same
temperament and appearance. They had the same number
of children of the same sex, lost and brought up the same
number; and even in the minor matters of life, as when
the clergyman turned from curate to rector, the shepherd
changed from sheep boy to chief herdsman.

I wish I knew the end of that story. I wonder if the two
old friends, who had been born at the same time and who
had shared unknowingly so many of life's experiences, met
death at the same time and in the same way. I daresay they
did.

Frequently, the differences in the charts of people born
approximately at the same time are quite as marked as the
similarities, and—as in the case of the twins—constitute
equally convincing proofs of the truth of astrology. As I
write, my mind turns to the case of two well-known men,
both clients of mine, who were born on the same day and
whose charts present some very remarkable aspects of an
almost twin-like character. One is an editor and the other

is a writer; and an interesting thing about their case is that neither can boast of any literary forbears. Yet both have made real successes in literary work.

Of course, to an astrologer, the reason is very simple. Both men have Mercury, the planet which rules the mind, in the sensitive, impressionable sign Pisces, in aspect to Mars, Saturn, Neptune and Uranus. Mars gives energy, Saturn gives industry, Neptune gives vision, and Uranus gives originality. No wonder these gentlemen have an unusual mentality, and no wonder they are not happy unless they are expressing it! Their Moon, ruling their relations with the public, is in the sturdy sign Taurus in conjunction with Jupiter, ruling money and success; so it was also inevitable that they should prosper, as they have done, through the operations of their most unusual Mercury.

Both men have Venus in Aries in aspect to Mars, which gives them great physical magnetism and makes them attractive to the opposite sex. Here, however, the resemblance ceases, and their dissimilarity becomes as much a proof of astrology's infallibility as their similarity. The two men were born on the same day, but *not* at the same hour and *not* in the same place. In the one case Sagittarius was rising at the hour of birth; in the other, Cancer. In the one case, Mars, the planet which shares with Venus the dominion over affairs of the heart, and is also a disrupting influence in the marital relations, is in the house of matrimony—*and the man with Mars so placed has had three wives!* In the other case, Mars is rising but unfriendly to Venus, a condition which usually gives many love affairs but only one wife—and *this* man with Mars *so* placed has just celebrated his twenty-fifth wedding anniversary!

And still there *are* those who do not believe that the stars influence man!

DOWN THROUGH THE AGES

SOME HISTORIC EXAMPLES

IN writing about my favorite subject, I usually stick fairly closely to incidents which have come under my own observation. Sometimes I wonder if I do not follow this policy too far. I remember the little boy in the pew who heard the minister read that eloquent passage from the Bible in which so many sentences begin with "I, John, saw." After a while he edged over beside his mother and whispered: "Who saw it besides John?" So, in this chapter, I am going to give you instances of astrology's infallibility most of which occurred before I was born!

I was particularly impressed with the necessity of giving this touch of impersonality to our consideration of the science by a letter I received not long ago, which began as follows: "Why haven't I heard of astrology before? Is it something you have invented yourself?"

Of course, to one who has spent her life in the study of this most ancient of all the sciences, it seems hardly possible that *anyone* should think that astrology was an invention of any living person or that anyone should *not* be familiar with the origin and history of the study of the stars. But, lest there be others who do not know the age and authority behind our present knowledge of planetary influences, I will quote from a scholarly work—but not too scholarly in the dull sense!—by the eminent British authority, C. J. S. Thompson.

"From the remote age when the Akkadians and the Sumerians began to observe the heavenly bodies and attempted to

trace their courses," Dr. Thompson writes, "till the time
when the Babylonians and the Egyptians began to attribute
to them certain powers over human beings and their destinies,
astrology wielded an important influence over kings and empires. (In those days, as Maspero puts it, 'Astrology was
the mistress of the world.') There seems little doubt that
astrology had its birth in Chaldea. In fact, the very name
Chaldean became synonymous with the word astrologer.
Even as late as the time of Alexander the Great, the Chaldean
astrologers were held in high esteem and regarded as men of
importance.

"The passage in St. Matthew where the wise men say, 'We
have seen his star,' points to a belief in a particular star indicating a birth. In Bethlehem, said the prophet, should be
born a saviour and we have seen his star in the East. The
astrologers or wise men (the names were synonymous in those
days) probably arrived six hours after the birth, when the
star had reached the meridian of Bethlehem. How they drew
their deductions from which they made their prediction is
a mystery, but that they were able to foretell certain events
in a remarkable way is proved by the early records. For
example, many of the official records of the early astrologers
of Nineveh and Babylon are still extant among the clay tab-
lets now preserved in the British Museum. (Some of the
Nineveh predictions probably date back to the time of Sar-
gon, the First—about five thousand years ago!)

"It can also be proved beyond doubt that the Greeks cast
horoscopes, which they drew up by certain rules according
to the astronomical state of the heavens at the moment of
a child's birth, and from them judged the fate and fortune
of its future. A Greek horoscope written on papyrus in the
first century is preserved in the British Museum.

"And, of course, everybody who read Shakespeare's 'Julius
Cæsar' during his school days remembers how the Romans

swore by astrology. Spurinna was the name of the astrologer who warned Cæsar to beware of the Ides of March, for on that day he would be in danger, but if he took care of himself he would be well. On March 15th, Cæsar decided that he would not leave the house, but on the persuasion of Brutus he was induced to go to the Senate, on the way to which he again met the astrologer. 'Well,' said Cæsar to him, 'the Ides of March are here and nothing has happened to me. You see your prediction is false.' 'True,' replied Spurinna, 'the day has arrived, *but it is not over yet.*' Within a few hours, Cæsar had received his mortal blow from the hand of his trusted friend!

"The Emperor Nero had several astrologers, but apparently his favorite was Babilus whom he often consulted. He is said to have put to death all whose horoscopes Babilus predicted would become powerful, or those he had reason to believe would become rivals and aspire to the throne. Characteristically, he afterward killed all the astrologers within his reach, so that none should be able to foretell the future Emperor!"

The practitioners of the art apparently passed through a trying time about this period, for if their patrons found their horoscopes inauspicious, they were often put to the torture or even death. That's something twentieth century astrologers are not obliged to cope with! Our clients sometimes *complain* if we tell them the truth, but they don't put us to death—at least, they haven't yet!

I could go on indefinitely for the benefit of my young friend who has just discovered astrology; and the answer would invariably be the same: in all ages, men have lived by the science of astrology. We know, for instance, that Napoleon continually consulted his stars. But Napoleon made a common mistake of followers of astrology. He believed in the stars, and he accepted and acted according to astrological conditions so long as they were favorable, but when they indicated that he had reached the limit of his success, he simply couldn't believe it.

Many years before the Battle of Waterloo, a well-known astrologer predicted that if ever Wellington and Napoleon should meet on the same battlefield, Wellington would inevitably win, because Wellington had Jupiter in that part of the heavens ruling honor and success, whereas Napoleon had Saturn in the same position. And it is true that in the year of Napoleon's downfall, Saturn was in a most unfavorable position to his Moon—and he knew it. He withdrew to let matters take their course, but he didn't wait long enough. The stars were still against him when he forced on the Battle of Waterloo and was routed. If Napoleon had waited,—well, I might have been writing this chapter in French instead of English!

But to go on with our historical examples: In the sixteenth century, a European astrologer, who was also an astronomer, made a careful study of a comet that flashed across the skies in a certain year. As a result, the astronomer, whose name was Tycho Brahe, published an announcement that in the North, in Sweden, there should be born a great king who would conquer Germany and then disappear in the year 1632. Sweden was the last place in which anybody expected a conquering king to be born. It was at that time a small, unimportant country. But Gustavus Adolphus, King of Sweden and later called "The Lion of the North," *did* overrun Germany and lay it waste, and died, as the astrologer had predicted in 1632.

Not only that but when he was at the height of his triumph, another astrologer, one of his own countrymen, went so far as to name the very day in 1632 on which he would be in danger of losing his life, just as the Roman astrologer warned Julius Cæsar of the Ides of March. And like Julius

Cæsar, Gustavus disregarded the warning. On the day of his affliction, he rode to the aid of his troops who were being hard pressed, became separated from his followers, and, riding almost alone in a squadron of the enemy, was fatally wounded and fell.

And even *that* is not all! He died at the time of day the astrologer had prophesied, 3:17 P.M. to be exact, and of the kind of blow the astrologer had foreseen, a wound in the eye. And a careful calculation of his horoscope today shows exactly the danger of which the wise man had warned him. I would have done the same thing if I had been alive and had read his horoscope in time.

Now if there were only a *few* such things on record, we might agree to blame "coincidence," which is a favorite word with a good many people who refuse to accept astrology's findings. But there are *thousands upon thousands* of such examples of the unfailing accuracy of astrological prediction when it is based on scientific calculation. Fifteen years before the great plague in London—we've all read about it in our history books—the event was predicted by William Lilly, a famous astrologer of the time. When it was all over, the House of Commons, which had calmly disregarded the prediction, sent for Lilly and asked his scientific aid in discovering who set the fire that started all the trouble. I know just how Lilly must have felt! When I have warned people against doing certain things at certain times, and they persist in doing them, that is all right; that is their business; or, as the phrase goes, "their hard luck." But when the same people come back to me for advice as to how to get out of their difficulties then I *am* at the end of my patience.

I fear I am not as long-suffering as I should be with disbelievers. And after reading this chapter of historic examples, you may sympathize with me. In this connection, I always think of a client I once had way back in the "mauve decade" who was torn between desire to profit by the teachings of the stars and conscientious objections to all matters which he could not understand. His chief reason for disbelieving astrology, so he said, was that he felt he had no right to anticipate the Lord's works. One pleasant day he arrived at my studio with a green alpaca umbrella and goloshes. This was too good an opportunity for me to miss. "Why," I asked, "are you carrying an umbrella?" "Oh," he replied, quite unsuspectingly, "I thought it looked like rain." "Shame on you," I said. "It was not raining when you left home, and you had no right to anticipate the workings of the Lord!"

Of course, I lost a client. But my position was a sound one. This weakling, by putting on his goloshes, had gone just as far as his limited knowledge permitted. The astrologer, in looking further into the future, profits by her greater knowledge of planetary law. The weakling reaches his limit in the possession of a green umbrella. The astrologer knows no limit but the Infinite!

But I promised you history in this chapter, not philosophy —and you shall have it. My first preceptor in astrology, Dr. J. Heber Smith (who wasn't a professional astrologer at all, but a great diagnostician and professor of materia medica at Boston University) gave me many examples of astrology's truth, one of which insists on being recalled at this time. It has to do with the "accidental conditions" which prevail from time to time in the horoscopes of all of us. An old philosopher, who was also an astrologer—as all wise men were in the ancient days—saw in his chart that he was likely to suffer death through something falling on him; so, being a wise-man, he tried to think of some way that he could avoid being in a position where anything *could* fall on him. He finally hit upon the sands of the seashore as an absolutely safe place; and putting his book under his arm, he went out and took a position well away from the water and with nothing over him but the blue sky. But his stars were too much for him. His time had come—and it came in the way predicted by his chart. An eagle with a scorpion in his beak, flying by, saw the bald pate of the old philosopher, took it for a rock, dropped the scorpion on the old man's head and instantly killed him.

"Well, that is a good fish story," I said to Dr. Smith. But he replied, as he did in all cases where I doubted his proofs of the infallibility of astrology, by going to his library shelves and quoting me "chapter and verse" for everything he had said. In fact, I have never found anyone to contradict the truth of this story—except that some people to whom I have told it insist that the thing which fell on the old man's head was not a scorpion but a tortoise. Some also object to my saying that the eagle was carrying anything at all in his beak because eagles carry things in their claws. Perhaps they are right: I am an astrologer, not a biologist or an ornithologist. About the only eagle I know much about is the one on the back of a twenty-five cent piece—and I am not so familiar with that as I should like to be! But the point of the story is *not* what the eagle dropped or how he dropped it, but that it *did* drop at the time the philosopher's horoscope said it would.

I can give you an even more remarkable instance of the way those "accidental conditions" pursue their victims. But this time I won't take any chances with my memory. I will quote verbatim from a well-known book, Wilson's "Life of Congreve"—and if the old-fashioned English sounds queer, don't blame me. It's not mine; it's the author's.

"The poet Dryden," so the tale runs, "had three sons, Charles, John and Henry. A very short time before Charles, his eldest son, was born, he laid his watch upon the table, and begged one of the ladies present in the most solemn man-

ner to take exact notice of the very minute the child was
born, which she did and acquainted him with it. About a
week after, when his lady was pretty well recovered, Mr.
Dryden took occasion to tell her that he had been casting
the child's nativity, and observed with regret that he had
been born in an evil hour. 'If he lives to arrive at his eighth
year,' said he, 'he will go near to die a violent death on his
very birthday, but if he should escape, as I see small hopes,
he will in his twenty-third year be under the same evil direction, and if he should escape that also, the thirty-third or
thirty-fourth year is, I fear . . . !' Here he was interrupted
by the immoderate grief of his lady, who could no longer
hear the calamity prophesied to befall her son.

"The time at last came, and August was the inauspicious
month in which young Dryden was to enter into the eighth
year of his age. His father had to go hunting on this day,
but bethinking himself of the child's horoscope, he took care
to set the boy a Latin exercise, with a strict charge not to
stir out of the room until his return. Charles was perform-
ing his duty in obedience to his father, but as ill-fate would
have it, the stag which the hunters were following made toward the house, and the noise alarming the servants, they
hastened out to enjoy the sport. One of the servants took
young Dryden by the hand and led him out to see it also,
but just as they came to the gate, the stag, being at bay with
the dogs, made a bold push and leaped over the court wall,
which was very low and very old, and the dogs following
threw down a part of the wall ten yards in length, under
which young Charles Dryden was found buried. He was
immediately dug out and revived, and after languishing six
weeks, he recovered. So far, Dryden's prediction was veri-
fied.

"In the twenty-third year of his age, Charles fell from
the top of an old tower belonging to the Vatican in Rome,

occasioned by a swimming in his head with which he was seized, the heat of the day being excessive. He again recovered, but was ever afterward in a languishing sickly state. In the thirty-third year of his age, being returned to England, he was unhappily drowned at Windsor. He had, with another gentleman, swum twice across the Thames, but returning a third time it was supposed he was taken with the cramp, because he called out for help, though too late. Thus the father's calculations proved but too prophetical."

I mention this story, as I did the one about the scorpion— or tortoise, or whatever it was!—merely to show the infallibility of the stars. But I wouldn't have you think because of these stories that I imbue my clients with the doctrine of fatality. For I do nothing of the kind. It is seldom indeed that the horoscope indicates any such sure danger as it must have in these two cases. Usually, the mere knowledge that we are under accidental conditions, and the ordinary precautions we take as a result of that knowledge, are all that is necessary to protect us from these conditions. As Henley says:

> *"It matters not how strait the gate,*
> *How charged with punishment the scroll,*
> *I am the master of my fate,*
> *I am the Captain of my Soul!"*

THE END